Tales for the Telling

50 SHORT STORIES FOR ASSEMBLIES

Written by
Kay McManus

First published
April 04 in Great Britain by

Educational Printing Services Limited

Albion Mill, Water Street, Great Harwood, Blackburn BB6 7QR
Telephone: (01254) 882080   Fax: (01254) 882010
e-mail: enquiries@eprint.co.uk   web site: www.eprint.co.uk

© Kay McManus 2004

ISBN 1 904374 76 X

Contents:

A Helping Hand

I've never liked Darren Smith much, but we're in the same class so I have to see him every day. I hate bullies, and Darren goes around pushing everyone out of his way just because he's bigger than the rest of us. From the start, I've never liked him, although since yesterday, I'm not sure how I feel about him.

I'm always supposed to go straight home after school, but mum doesn't mind if I sometimes stop at my friend Tom's house on the way back. He has far more computer games than I have, and mum knows she can always check if I'm there. Anyway, it was really hot when we came out of school yesterday, and Tom suggested that we went into the little wood beyond the railway station which has a small pond and a stream where you can make bridges.

As I was standing there making my mind up, Darren Smith rushed by, nearly knocking me over.

"Did you see that?" I said to Tom. "He's always doing that."

"Never mind him," Tom said. "Are you coming or not?" Then he ran off down the road towards the station. I always like being with Tom so I started to follow, but then I saw a car pull in just beside him. I recognised Tom's dad and I wasn't surprised when Tom turned around to wave at me and then got into the car. I'd met his dad and I knew Tom had to do what he was told, or there would be trouble, so I couldn't blame him for not going to the wood as he'd planned.

But once I'd started thinking about the stream and the little pond, I didn't feel like going home straight away, so I still went over the railway crossing towards the path that leads to the wood. It's one of those crossings where a barrier goes down when a train comes, and most of the time you can get on to the railway line quite easily. That was when I saw Darren. He was on his own further along the track, and at first I thought he was just bending to pick something up.

Then he saw me and shouted, "I can't move! I'm stuck!"

I thought he meant he'd trapped his foot, but as I ran up to him he said, "It's my ankle. I had an operation last year and it's always giving way. I think I've broken it again. I tripped over the rail."

It was then I heard the bell ring at the crossing, which meant there was a train on the way. I saw from his face that he had heard it too. I couldn't believe what I was seeing. Darren Smith was crying! The bully we all hated was actually crying.

I pretended I hadn't noticed. "Come on - lean on me," I said. "You'll be O.K. if we get you up on the bank."

I had to take nearly all his weight, so it was a struggle to steer him to the bank but instead of sitting down he said, "I only live down there. Can we make it?"

He was pointing towards the house at the crossing. It had once been part of the old signal box, but it had been repaired, and now there were window boxes and lots of new paint, so I knew someone must have bought it. I looked at Darren in amazement. How could he be so lucky? If I'd lived in that house, with the trains rushing past my bedroom window, I would have told everybody about it. But Darren had never mentioned it.

The train passed us just as we opened a private gate into the railway house. Darren had stopped sniffing now. "Want to come inside? Dad's got a lot of stuff from the old railway house if you'd like to see it."

Then he hesitated. "Don't tell anyone about this, will you? Maybe I've only just twisted my ankle, but it did hurt."

I knew he was remembering how he'd cried and had made such a fuss about the pain, so I promised that I wouldn't. His house was fantastic. There were so many things to look at, like old photographs and things from the signal box. I didn't have enough time to look at them all, but Darren says I can go again any time I like. The funny thing is I think he meant it, and I was pleased this morning before school when he came up to me to show me his ankle all strapped up. He won't be able to rush around quite so much now, pushing everyone out of the way, and perhaps he might not even want to.

PRAYER:

Help me to take time in getting to know the people I meet before I start judging them.

Pass It On!

My friend Amy never stops talking, and most of the time her stories are all about other people. Miss Johnson, our teacher, says that Amy would win first prize if there was ever a competition for finding the best way of wasting time, but I like hearing her talk because she makes me laugh. Her stories are mostly about things that have happened at school; they spread around the class, and by the end of the day, everybody knows about them. Sometimes, though, she goes all serious and says she has a secret that she can only tell me when we're on our own. Then she takes me to the end of the playground and always says the same thing. "I've got a special secret. Would you like to know what it is?"

Sometimes I try and pretend that I don't, but in the end I generally say 'yes', and she always glances around to make sure nobody else is listening and speaks in a whisper to make it sound important. Most times the things she tells me when we're alone aren't any more exciting than the ones she tells everybody else, but being told one of these particular secrets somehow makes you feel special because you know something that nobody else knows.

But last week one of these special secrets was about Tracey, who has been my best friend since the first day we started school, so when I listened to what Amy was telling me, I just couldn't believe it.

"But Tracey would never steal anything," I said. "She would never do that!"

Amy moved closer. "But it's true. I saw her myself. She took three big chocolate bars. She must have thought the shop was empty, but I was behind the magazines. She walked right along the counter looking, and then she took the bars quickly and put them in her school bag. Three whole bars - can you believe it!"

We had to go inside then, but all day I went on thinking about Tracey. I even told two other people because I wanted to hear them agree with me that she would never have done such a thing. I heard later that they'd told two other people as well, and I felt sorry that I'd not kept Amy's secret. I began to wonder how many others might have heard about it by now, perhaps even Tracey herself? Or the Headteacher? If what Amy said was true, then Tracey would soon be in serious trouble.

I hardly slept that night thinking of what I should do, but the next morning I saw Tracey waiting for me by the school gates. I tried to pretend I hadn't seen her, but she came running across to me.

"Sorry - I meant to give you this before," she said, and before I could speak, she took out a big chocolate bar from her schoolbag and put it into my hand.

"I've been given three," she said. "My auntie owns the corner shop and she says they're a prize for winning that race at the fete last Saturday. She had a phone call just as we were talking, so she told me to help myself to three of anything I liked. I chose these because I know they're your favourites. I've given one to mum and I'm keeping the other for myself."

I couldn't think of anything to say. Tracey is my best friend and I should have known that she would never steal things just because she wants them. Because of what Amy and I had done, the story might be going around the whole school even now. I looked down at the chocolate bar and then back at Tracey.

"What's the matter?" she said. "Aren't you going to eat it right away like you always do?"

"No, I think I'll save it for a bit," I said, "to remind me."

Tracey looked puzzled. "Remind you?"

"Not to listen to secrets," I said, "especially when they're about your best friend."

So in future I never shall - and I have decided about the chocolate bar too. I will go to Amy during break and offer to share it with her. I can't wait to see her face when I tell her the truth. It will almost be worth being able to eat only half of Tracey's prize!

PRAYER:

Please help me to remember that our words can damage other people and are out of our control as soon as they are spoken.

Bully For You!

Ben is the biggest boy in the school and he knows it. Because everybody is much smaller than he is, he likes to make them do things like picking up his books if he drops them, or making everybody move out of his way when he comes into the classroom. As you might guess, he doesn't have many friends.

I always try to avoid him as much as I can because he picks on me all the time. Mum keeps asking me if I'm worried about anything at school. She says I rush away from the school gates as if I were trying to hide from somebody.

"You're not being bullied, are you?" she says. "Because if you are you must tell somebody."

But I didn't tell her about Ben as I thought he might find out, which would make things worse than they were already. Nor did I tell mum about the dreams I keep having. They're all the same really. I'm standing at the top of a high tower and Ben is behind me trying to push me off. I know I've got to jump, and sometimes I'm already plunging down through space towards the ground - which is when I usually wake up. I know they're only dreams, but each day at school seems to give Ben another chance to push me around, and the dreams are getting worse.

One of his recent tricks is to get me into a corner and say that I've stolen something of his. It was awful yesterday because I knew he'd lost his pen and that he'd accuse me of stealing it, so I made sure I kept out of his way until it was time to go home.

It felt great to be safely away from school and to know that I didn't have to go back there until the next day, and I felt really good when I went up to my bedroom. I like being on my own up there because it's an attic room, and it has a tiny round window like a port-hole which makes me feel as if I'm on a ship. But I'd only just settled down to read when I heard mum coming upstairs.

"I've just had a visitor," she said. "Mrs Nichols from down the road. I've never met her before but she came round collecting for the church roof, and we had a nice chat while I was looking for my purse."

I tried to look interested but mum's stories can sometimes go on and on, and I couldn't understand why she'd come all the way up two lots of stairs just to tell me about someone collecting for the church roof. But by now she was sitting beside me on the bed so I knew she was going to be there for a long time.

"She's apparently having an awful time at the moment," she went on. "Her oldest son Greg is in prison for an armed robbery. Even when he was young he had to go into care because he was so violent. Even his young brother was frightened of him, but at least now Greg's in prison, life's a bit easier for Ben. Mrs Nichols says you're in the same class and she says it would be nice if you could be friends. You've never mentioned anyone called Ben. Do you know him?"

I stared at her. "I know a Ben Nichols but he's not my friend, mum." I couldn't imagine someone like Ben having a big brother he was afraid of. It suddenly made me see him quite differently. Perhaps he sometimes had bad dreams too.

"Anyway," said mum, "it sounds as if he could do with a few friends, so do your best."

For the first time ever, I didn't have the dream about the tower that night, and when I saw Ben at school the next day, I didn't feel half as scared as I generally did. And when he came up to me in the playground and said he still couldn't find his pen, I didn't even try to run away.

"Not to worry," I said. "I'll lend you one of mine." And that, I thought, was friendly enough even to please mum, and it certainly surprised Ben!

PRAYER:

Help me to remember that bullies are not always as brave as they pretend to be.

Sand Between My Toes

My brother Steve has always said that he'd like to live by the sea, and he still says it even after what happened this year when we went to Golden Bay. We go there every year because mum has a friend who has a caravan on the cliff top and she lets us use it every August. It's great on the first day of each holiday when we go down the little path from the caravan and find that everything looks just as it did the year before.

But this year there was something a bit different. There was a new notice stuck on a board at the end of the path, and mum said it was very important that we remembered to do what it said, which was not to go to the far end of the beach.

Apparently, during the winter storms, some of the cliff had crumbled and fallen, so now it was dangerous to go beyond the rocks where we always paddled and looked for shrimps.

"Even at high tide there's plenty of sand for you to play on," said mum, "so there's no need to go further along the beach."

When we are on holiday, mum and dad like to go for long walks into the next bay. Steve and I can't wait to be on our own to play on what we pretend is our own beach. I like being on holiday with him because we don't argue as much as we do at home. Every day we go down to the beach, and each day time seems to go faster and faster, until we realise it is our very last day at Golden Bay.

It was the first morning that the sun wasn't shining. There was a cold wind that whipped up the sand and knocked over the café chairs, so mum and dad decided not to walk very far. We were glad when at last they were out of sight.

"We haven't caught one single shrimp this year," said Steve. "Come on, let's have another try."

It's funny how easily you can forget the time when you're looking for shrimps, but when I felt some rain on my arm, I looked up and realised we had walked almost to the end of the beach. Then, in the next moment, there was a roaring sound from the cliff behind us. Rocks and rubble came crashing down, scattering across the sand and into the sea. There was no longer any space for us to walk back along the beach!

Steve grabbed my hand. "We'll have to scramble back over the rocks - come on!"

I could see a big wave rushing towards us, as another fall of rocks crashed down and hit the beach. Then suddenly, through the rain, I saw dad climbing over the rocks towards us. He was shouting, raising his arm as if to stop us.

"Emma! Steve! Stay where you are. I'm coming!"

I have never been so glad to grab his hand, and I didn't even notice that Steve already had, as if he would never let him go. Slowly and carefully, dad helped us over the fallen rocks until at last we were on firm sand again. People were running towards us from the café, and we saw mum rushing to join them, waving to us as she ran.

That night, after we'd had our hot drinks and had settled down in our bunks, we lay and listened to the sound of the wind and the rain clattering on the caravan roof. Mum and dad stayed up late, and I listened to them talking for a long time, though they were speaking quietly and I couldn't hear what they were saying. I would have liked to have known because they were quiet at breakfast too and never said anything about how Steve and I had forgotten what that notice had said. But I knew they must have been thinking how lucky we'd been because that is what I'm still thinking, even now, when we've come home again and I'm back in my own bed.

I don't think I want to go back to the seaside again, at least not for a while. But if we do go next August, there'll be no need to remind us about that notice.

PRAYER:

Help me to remember that although rules sometimes stop us doing what we want to do, they are there to keep us safe.

Moving Day

They'd marked the day on the calendar that hung on the kitchen wall. Kevin had drawn a big red ring round the date so there was no way Joanna could forget about it.

"I'm not likely to forget that we're going to move, am I?" said Joanna. "No one ever talks about anything else these days."

Kevin didn't seem to mind that Moving Day was getting really close now. At first Joanna hadn't believed it when mum had said they were going, but it looked now as if nothing would stop it happening. She still hated the whole idea. She loved their little house. Her Mum told her that she was born there, and that as a baby she had slept in her pram on the lawn. Of course, Joanna couldn't remember that, but she knew every inch of the garden, almost as well as she knew each room of the house. She also knew everybody in the street. There were the Ahmeds next door, and the Simpsons on the other side, as well as the Browns and the Turners. In fact, she knew everybody, and she and Kevin had lots of friends who went to the same school and lived close by.

Now, because of dad's new job, everything was going to change. They would have to go to a different school in a different town and never see any of their old friends again.

When Moving Day finally arrived, it was worse than she'd expected. Dad grumbled all the time, and mum fussed and worried because half the furniture didn't fit into the new flat. Even Kevin wasn't in a good mood, so Joanna was pleased when at last it was bedtime. Mum had tried to close the curtains but there was a big gap in the middle because they were too small.

"You'll have to manage with these for the moment," she said, "but it's not as if anybody can see us up here." She switched out the light and bustled out again without stopping to talk as she generally did.

"I wish we could go home again, where nothing has changed," Joanna thought. "Why couldn't everything have stayed the same?"

She tossed and turned, stretched and wriggled, and still she couldn't sleep. Perhaps, she thought, if I could close the curtains a bit more . . . and she got out of bed and went to the window. Peering through the gap in the curtains, she saw the whole town sparkling with lights. It was as if someone had thrown a handful of diamonds into the darkness far below. Joanna gasped in surprise. Being in a flat on the ninth floor of a tall building was much more exciting than being in a little house in a row of other little houses!

She opened the curtains wider. Gradually she began to recognise different patterns of lights. A long curving string of them marked the end of the motorway where the removal van had carried everything from their old house, and she could see the moving lights of cars as they flowed between the lines of lights. Above her head was the wide expanse of sky and a moon half hidden with clouds. It was almost as good as when they'd flown to Scotland to stay with Gran, but even better because close by was her own warm bed.

Then the door opened and mum came in. "I didn't think you were in bed!" she said. "I've just had a visit from our new neighbours. Apparently they have two girls about your age who are going to come round tomorrow to show you the playground where there are slides and swings for all the children who live in the flats."

"You never told me there was a playground here," said Joanna.

"You never listened," said mum. "You said you didn't want to hear anything about our new home."

Joanna knew that this was true, so to change the subject she quickly said, "Come and have a look at all these lights, mum."

So mum looked at the lights and agreed that it was almost as good as flying, but she said that it was very late and that she was off to bed. "You must be tired too," she said.

"Not really," said Joanna. "But then I've always liked moving."

PRAYER:

*Change often feels like the ending of something. Help me
to see that it's really a new beginning.*

Keeping a Secret

Do you like being told a secret? Kirsty always hoped that one of her friends at school would tell her a really exciting one, but they never did.

Then one day, she made a new friend. Her name was Donna, and she told Kirsty that her family had only just moved down from Scotland. Everybody seemed to like her because she made them laugh, and Kirsty thought she was the most interesting friend she had ever had. They sat together whenever they could, and soon Kirsty felt she knew everything about Donna's two brothers, her new baby sister, and about her father who drove big trucks all over the country.

Sometimes, though, Donna would go very quiet and tell Kirsty that she didn't feel like talking or being with anybody. On days like this, Kirsty felt hurt because it made Donna seem like a stranger again.

"Is something wrong?" she would say to her new friend. "Why can't you tell me? If it's a secret, I promise I won't tell anyone."

Generally Donna would say it was nothing, until one day, she told Kirsty that she did have something very secret to tell her.

"You must swear not to tell anyone," she said. "I'm going back to Scotland on my own. Nobody will miss me because they're all too busy fussing over the baby."

Kirsty was horrified. "You mean you're going to run away?"

"I know how to get there. But you don't need to know anything else."

In one way, Kirsty was pleased that she now had a real secret to keep, but she wished Donna had told her a lot more. When was she going? Where would she live? What would her parents do when she disappeared?

Kirsty began to worry about all these questions, and she felt even worse when one morning she went to school and there was no sign of Donna. All that week, she waited for news of her, trying to think of how she would answer all the questions. She would have to lie and say, "No, she didn't tell me where she was going, and she never told me she was going to run away."

But nothing seemed to be happening. At last she plucked up courage and asked her teacher if she had heard if Donna was ill, and was relieved to be told that she was, and that she would be coming back to school on the following Monday.

However, during the next week there was still no sign of Donna, and on Wednesday evening, Kirsty's mother told her that nobody knew where Donna was. She had definitely gone missing.

Kirsty hardly slept that night. She knew that, sometimes, dreadful things happened to girls like Donna, because she had seen how their parents cried when they came on television to ask for information about their daughters. Until now, she had kept her promise to Donna and had told no one else about the secret, but if anything happened to her friend now, she knew that it would be her fault.

By morning, Kirsty decided she had no choice but to break her promise. With her heart pounding, she went straight to Donna's house before school. The house looked as it always did, and Donna's mother came to the door, wiping her hands on a tea towel as though she was washing up on an ordinary morning.

"Scotland?" she said. "Well, thank you for telling me, Kirsty. But I'm afraid she never got there. We found her last night at the coach station. She hadn't enough money to go very far so she slept on a bench in the park. We didn't realise she was so upset about moving here, and she didn't tell us what she was planning to do. But Donna's fine now, and I'm sure she'll be back at school in the morning."

"You won't tell her that I broke my promise, will you?" said Kirsty.

"I shan't say a word, and thanks again, Kirsty."

So Kirsty and Donna are friends again, and neither of them has ever mentioned Scotland or about Donna running away. But if anyone comes to Kirsty now to tell her a secret, she just doesn't want to know!

PRAYER:

Sometimes it is difficult to keep secrets so help me not to make too many promises that I can't keep.

Yours and Mine

Everybody in the school knows Andy Browning. He has so many friends round him that you can always see where he is in the playground. I think people like him because he makes jokes about himself and is always giving things away. You've only got to tell him that you like his penknife or a book he's reading and he'll say you can have it. I suppose it's because he has an uncle who is always buying him things, so he knows he won't have to wait very long before he gets another present. Most of us don't have uncles like that. At least I don't, but mum is always telling me that having things doesn't make you any happier.

"Cheer up, Linda," she says. "You'd be much happier if you stopped wanting what other people have."

Mum's always saying that and it generally makes me feel worse. Anyway, this afternoon I decided to ask Andy about the new video he'd just been given. I knew he'd got the new one with him because he told us it was in his schoolbag, but instead of saying that I could have it, as he usually did, he just said, "Sorry, not now."

"Can I come round to your house to watch it tonight then?" I said. But before he could answer, I heard Miss Barlow calling to him to come to the staff room before he went home.

Andy said, "Bother!" and dropped his schoolbag where we were standing by the cloakroom door.

That's when I did something really bad. I told myself that he wouldn't mind if I only borrowed it for one night. I felt sure that was what he would have said if he'd had time to answer me. After all, I was his friend and he'd given or lent me so many things. Surely he'd understand?

Things went well at first. I looked round to see if anyone else was in the cloakroom and reached into his school bag to find the video. It was wrapped in a brown paper bag and he'd pushed it right to the bottom, but I managed to fish it out from among all his books, and I tucked it under my jacket and hoped I wouldn't meet anyone at the school gate.

I was just hanging up my jacket at home when mum came into the hall. "What's this then?" she said, picking up the video from the chair.

"It's only a video. Andy's lent it me. Just for tonight." I must have gone red or something because mum gave me a funny look and took the video out of its bag.

"You say this is Andrew's?" she said.

"It's from his uncle. He's always buying him things."

"Has his mother seen it?" mum said.

"I don't know," I said. I couldn't understand why she was making such a fuss. She'd never minded me watching videos before.

"I'm sorry, Linda," she said. "I'm going to ring his mother right away. Andy is older than you and he should not have given you this."

I didn't know what to say. How could I have been so stupid to do something I'd never done before? Just because I'd stolen Andy's video, it seemed we were both going to be in serious trouble.

"Please don't, mum," I said. "I'll take it back to him in the morning. He doesn't know I've got it. I took it from his bag. But I'll tell him, I promise."

I waited for mum to say something, but the silence seemed to go on and on as mum looked down at the video. Then she said, "I still might have a word with Andy's mother later. I think this video was stolen with a whole lot of others. I read about it in the local paper and remembered the label. It's meant for grown-ups, Linda, and wherever Andy's uncle got it from, it's not one he should have passed on to Andy."

I didn't really understand all she was saying, but suddenly I felt relieved that I had told her the truth. Tomorrow morning I'd give Andy his video back and hope that he would try and forgive me, and knowing Andy, I think he might. I'm quite glad now that I don't have an uncle like his . . . but I shan't tell him that.

PRAYER: ═══

Help me to remember that any bad action is likely to affect someone else.

Cross My Heart

Gran always says that I have a sweet tooth. I suppose it's because I love the pudding part of a meal, the part when grown-ups say, 'Oh no, I really shouldn't,' and then tuck into a big piece of sticky toffee pudding or cream trifle, like they haven't eaten for months.

The trouble is that Gran is such a good cook. Everything you eat in her house is somehow special, but then she spends ages in the kitchen, whereas mum has to fit in our meals with going out to work, and she's generally too tired to bother much when she comes home at night.

Of course, all three of us help as well - that's me, Laura, and my brothers, Stewart and Barry - but mum still likes to be in charge so it's not the same as doing it entirely on your own. But we all love going to Gran's. She always makes an extra surprise for us to bring home, like toffee apples or flapjacks. Mum often tells her that they're bad for our teeth, but Gran only laughs and says that mum has forgotten what it's like to be young.

You'd think Gran would have forgotten that years ago. She's so old, and lately she never makes us any surprises and often forgets things when she lays the table.

Last winter she had flu and had to go into hospital for a week. After that, she fell and broke her arm, and then a few months later, hurt herself trying to cut down some bushes in the garden. So for a few months we didn't go to her house for any meals. Instead, mum would make some sandwiches and take a flask of soup for us all so that we didn't cause Gran any extra work.

Last week, Gran suddenly decided that she wanted us all to go for Sunday dinner just like we used to do. At first, mum said it wasn't a good idea, but Gran looked so disappointed that in the end mum said that we would go, but we wouldn't stay too long afterwards so that Gran could have a nice afternoon rest. So on Sunday there we all were again, sitting around her big table. I thought Gran looked a bit tired right from the beginning, and mum had to carry all the big dishes of vegetables from the kitchen for her. But now Gran said she wanted to fetch the pudding herself.

"You sit still now," she said. "There's no need to fuss. I can manage."

She seemed to be a long time in the kitchen, and when she came back, she looked very worried.

"It's a new recipe," she said, "but I've lost my glasses and so I couldn't read it very clearly. I hope it will be all right. It took me all morning."

The pudding, which was meant to be some sort of sponge, was awful. We all tried a spoonful but that was enough! It was slimy and yet lumpy, and it tasted bitter and sickly at the same time. Gran saw our faces, and she looked as if she were going to cry. Stewart was giggling which he always does when he doesn't know what to say, and mum glared at him and said quickly, "It has a lovely cream topping, mum." Then she looked at me and I knew I had to say something too, so I made myself take another spoonful and said, "I like the cherries on it."
Gran suddenly snatched my dish. "The ground almonds must have gone off. I've had them in the cupboard for months, and I didn't beat the eggs enough. Don't eat any more - we'll just have some fruit instead."

She looked so sad that I said, "Can we come next Sunday too, Gran? It would be great if we could."

So Gran cheered up, and Stewart told us a lot of jokes he'd heard at school while we ate some apples, and in the end everything was all right again. But mum was very quiet coming home, and she says that she's going to suggest that Gran comes to live with us instead of being on her own, which I think is quite a good idea, and then we can choose the pudding.

PRAYER:

We can sometimes hurt people by bluntly telling them the truth.
Help me to remember to be particularly careful about the
feelings of those who are growing old.

Fighting Fit

Miss Jennings says she doesn't watch much television - apart from the news, of course. Miss Jennings is our teacher and she's always telling us to remember that all the things we see on our screens are only acted. They're not real. On a small television screen I think it's quite easy to remember that the actors are only pretending, even when you see them smash up furniture and drive cars into walls. But sometimes it's more difficult when you go to a cinema where there's a huge wide screen and the sounds are all around you. You feel as if it's all happening to you and that it's quite real, so I'm not sure that Miss Jennings is right all the time.

One day last week she asked us all to tell about one of our own adventures, but all I could think of was a fight I'd seen in a film that dad had taken me to see. When I get home after a film, I often go around to my friend Chris's house, and we act out the story all over again. Sometimes we go into the back lane where there are some old sheds and we have pretend fights and shoot each other like the two baddies in the film, so I was speaking the truth when I told the class that we went on fighting until it was dark.

I don't think Miss Jennings believed me at all.

"That's an exciting story, Grant," she said, "but we wanted to hear about something that's true, that actually happened to you. I don't suppose you really shot your friend, did you?"

Everybody laughed, and I said, "But we were in the back lane and that was real and so were the sheds. We go there a lot."

Another boy called Darren said he knew the sheds too, but Miss Jennings said she wasn't interested in talking about sheds, and could we hear someone else's story, as we hadn't much time.

Afterwards, Darren came up to me and asked if he could come with Chris and me next time we went into the lane. Neither of us really knew him and I wasn't too keen on him coming, but he and Chris soon began to hang around together, so in the end I said I didn't mind. It was a few weeks before we all saw another film with a fight in it, and Darren and Chris were keen to get started in the back lane. I still wished it could have been just Chris and me - especially when Darren began telling us what to do and where he wanted us to hide. I think he'd already forgotten that it was just a game because straight away he made a lunge at me and sent me flying. I must have hit my head on something and I was so mad that I struck back at his face. Then I felt something trickling down my neck and Chris said, "Stop it, Darren! Stop it! Grant's split his head open."

My cut wasn't as bad as it sounded, but I felt dizzy and sick, and I saw that Chris was frightened too.

"Did you see that? Darren was fighting for real!" he said.

Darren started to walk away saying that we were just a couple of stupid kids anyway, so Chris lent me his hankie and said we ought to be getting back.

"He really was fighting for real," he said again. "You should have seen his face when he hit you."

I wanted to tell him that I'd found myself fighting for real too because I felt so mad with Darren. But I didn't. Instead I just said, "It wasn't much of a film anyway, was it?"

And Chris agreed. That's the good thing about having friends.They know exactly what you mean without being told.

PRAYER:

Help me to remember that anger can easily turn into a wish to hurt someone else.

Weaving a Web

My little brother Mark has been a nuisance since the day he was born. He's always falling off chairs or down the stairs, and he takes the tyres off all his toy trucks and puts them in the sugar bowl just when I'm going to have my cereal. He often gets me into trouble too, even when it's not my fault, like the day he knocked over my hot chocolate and it went all over the table. I think some of it might have splashed him because he began to scream. Mum came running in from the kitchen. I knew she was really angry because that morning the washing machine had broken and the milkman hadn't left us enough milk.

"What on earth have you done to him now?" mum said. "Can't I leave you two alone for one minute?"

"*He* knocked it over," I said, "not me."

"But I told you to keep it out of his reach. That's why I put it on the tray instead of near him."

I didn't say anything because I'd forgotten that when I took the first sip I hadn't put it back on the tray. Mum looked so furious that I said quickly, "He's only three, mum. He didn't mean to."

She seemed to calm down then and went to fetch a towel to mop the tablecloth. Mark had stopped crying and seemed to have forgotten the whole thing, so I felt quite pleased that I'd thought of letting him take the blame for what really was my fault.

I've done the same thing quite a few times since then, so now, when there's trouble, mum just sighs and says, "I suppose it was Mark's fault, was it?" And I always say it was.

On Saturday my friend Helen came round to play in the garden. Of course we had to put up with Mark being there too, which was a nuisance. Helen had been given a new bracelet for her birthday and Mark wanted to have a look at it, so she let him try it on while she gave me a push on the swing. Then I tried it on too, while she pushed Mark, but it must have been a bit tight because when I took it off I had to tug really hard and it suddenly fell off my hand. I didn't know what to do and I didn't dare look at Helen. The bracelet broke as I tugged it off! How could I explain what I'd done when she'd just told us it was one of the nicest presents she'd ever had?

Picking up the bracelet again I said, "Mark must have broken it when he tried it on. It was like this when he gave it to me. He's always breaking things." But instead of believing me like mum does, Helen looked puzzled.

"But I saw you put it on and it was all right then. Look, it's only the catch. Unless you fasten it properly, it doesn't work. Anyway, Mark's wrist is so small that he didn't have to undo it when he put it on and took it off so you can't blame him. You were the one who used the catch, not him."

I looked across at my brother. Mark was swinging so high that he was nearly hidden in the branches of the apple tree, but when he swooped down I could see his face again. Swinging in the wind had made his face all red and shiny, and he was grinning and looked so happy that I was suddenly afraid that he would swing too high and fall.

"Be careful, Mark!" I shouted. "I'll come over and give you a push. Hang on tight!"

Helen looked surprised. "You don't generally fuss over him like that. You always say he's a nuisance."

I couldn't tell her why I wanted Mark to be safe, and why I suddenly felt so ashamed about blaming him for all those things he hadn't done. But I knew I didn't want to go on telling any more lies.

Speaking the truth at last I said, "He's not really a nuisance - at least not very often!"

PRAYER:

Help me to remember that telling one small lie often means we have to tell lots more.

It's Not My Turn

Toby had been living with the Jenkins family ever since he was a puppy. Dad had fetched him from the Dogs' Home and Hayley thought she had never seen anything so small and lonely before. Kim liked him too. For the first few months the girls couldn't wait to take Toby out for a walk on the common as soon as they got home from school. But he didn't stay a puppy for very long, and soon he was far too big to sit on their knees or even be picked up - which was when the girls began to argue about whose turn it was to take Toby out.

One day mum decided that they must have a rota pinned up on the kitchen cupboard door, and for a time the rota worked well. Toby looked really fit and happy and Hayley used to enjoy her turn of taking him out for his daily runs. Gradually though, the leaves began to fall off the trees and Hayley sometimes wished she could stay by the fire and watch television instead.

One afternoon, mum had taken Kim into town to buy some new shoes, and dad was busy in the shed making a shelf for the bathroom. Hayley's friend had lent her a video and she was looking forward to being able to see it on her own for once without anyone interrupting. But Toby seemed to know that it was time for his walk with Hayley, because he kept fetching his lead and pushing it on to her lap.

"Not now, Toby" she said. "Dad will take you tonight. It's starting to snow again and it will take me ages to put on my boots and gloves and everything. Go and lie down."

But Toby still wandered around the room looking sorry for himself, until in the end, Hayley switched off the video and went to the back door. As she opened it, a flurry of snow blew in and Toby gave a bark of excitement, leaping around her with delight. The air felt icy and Hayley could hardly see through the snowflakes to the end of the garden.

"Oh, go out for a minute then," she said. "We can't go for a walk in all this . . . but come back inside when I call you."

Toby had always been good at coming to heel as soon as he was called, so, feeling more cheerful, Hayley went back to the fireside again and switched on the video. It's very easy to forget how quickly time passes when you're watching an exciting film, so she was surprised to find the room had become quite dark when she suddenly remembered that she had let Toby out into the garden. Then suddenly, she heard the loud screeching of brakes. Almost at once she remembered the hole in the garden fence! Without pausing to snatch her coat, she ran outside, down the garden path and out into the road, calling to Toby as she ran. She could see that a car had stopped, and that something was lying in the snow beyond its headlights.

"Toby!" she called, as the driver of the car ran towards the body in the road.

"It's hard to see anything in this blizzard," the driver said. "The dog ran out before I could stop."

But Toby was already struggling to his feet, as dad came racing out of the house.

"Will he be all right, dad?" Hayley sobbed.

"He's a very lucky dog," dad said, "but I think we'd better get the vet to have a look at him."

Dad and Hayley walked slowly back into the house.

"You ought to have been home long before this," dad said. "And why wasn't Toby on his lead?"

Hayley knew that later she would have to explain everything, but for the moment, all that mattered was that Toby was all right. Later, when they'd had the vet's assurance that he had only been bruised, she made a secret promise, though it was a promise she thought no-one else had heard.

But as she whispered it to herself, Toby's ears seemed to twitch. After all, there was one special word he could always recognise, and that was the magic word 'walk'.

PRAYER:

*Help me to be caring about all the animals that live in our world
and to do nothing that will harm them.*

Joking Apart

It's always different when Neil isn't at school. He seems to be away a lot, and if there's anything going round the class like a bad cold or a cough, Neil's always the one who disappears first. I could understand it if he was like his brother, Paul, who has asthma, who, apart from having to use his nebulizer sometimes, seems to be fine.

Neil once told me that he was born too soon and was so small that they kept him in hospital for ages. I suppose that could make you catch colds more easily. He's certainly not as tall as the rest of us but he makes up for it by being noisier than anyone else. He's always saying things about people that make us laugh, and he can copy how people walk and how they speak and somehow makes it really funny, so that when you next see the actual person he's copying, you start to laugh straight away. Anyway, that's why everybody likes Neil.

One day last week, during break, I saw a big gang of people standing near the stage at the end of the hall. When I heard them laughing, I knew that Neil must be there somewhere. He was. He was speaking just like Shadi, a new boy who doesn't speak English very well. I like Shadi, but he's very different from Neil. I do like them both, even though Shadi is very quiet, and he always looks as if he's thinking of something else when the teacher asks him a question. When he does answer, he generally shakes his head and says, "I do not know Miss sorry," as if the teacher's name is Miss Sorry and he doesn't know her.

So when I heard Neil say again, "I do not know Miss sorry," it sounded so much like Shadi that for a moment I thought it was him. Then suddenly, I saw that he was there in the crowd, listening to the laughter. He looked puzzled at first, and then he started to walk away. I saw him a few minutes later, standing alone near the classroom door. I didn't have to say anything because he spoke first, but this time when I heard his voice, I didn't laugh.

"I speak English very bad," he said. "But why do they laugh?"

At first I didn't know what to say, and then I remembered something that had happened to me.

"Neil is always making people laugh," I said. "One day when I fell off my desk he showed everyone exactly what I had done, and they all laughed. I felt angry with him at first, but afterwards I realised that Neil is away from school so often, he finds it hard to keep up with the rest of us. When he makes us all laugh, he can forget all that and feel just the same as everybody else".

Shadi looked surprised. "He laughed at you, too?"

"He likes making people laugh, that's all. When you know him better, you'll understand."

Shadi still looked puzzled, so that afternoon when Neil and I were walking home from school, I said that Shadi couldn't help being clever and that it wasn't fair to laugh at him just because he was clever and knew more than one language.

"Clever?" Neil said. "He doesn't sound very clever."

"Well he is," I said, "because my mum works in the post office and Shadi came in once with some parcels that had to be sent overseas. Mum said he weighed them all, and worked out all the postage much faster than she could have done herself. And every one of them was exactly right."

Neil went very quiet then. I knew that he's hopeless at adding things up or doing any kind of sum and is always making mistakes when he tries to multiply anything.

"Next time you're coming to our house," I said, "I'll ask Shadi too, shall I? And you can show him how I fell off my desk."

And when he saw I was laughing, he laughed too, but I have a feeling that once he gets to know Shadi properly, he'll never laugh at him again.

PRAYER:

Help me not to hurt other people by laughing at them because they are different from me.

How Do I Look?

I sometimes go to my friend Debby's house. It's the largest one at the top of the hill, and it has a big garden with a pond and four fish. Debby hasn't any brothers or sisters so she likes coming home with me. I think my brothers are a nuisance most of the time but they're not too bad when Debby is with me. Mike, he's my oldest brother, hardly says a word to her, and he goes all red if he sees her looking at him.

Once, when we were on our own, I asked him if he really liked Debby and he said he wasn't bothered. But I know he is. He just stares and stares at her. I suppose I can see why, because she looks much prettier than all the other friends I've taken home.

I often tell mum that I wish my hair was like Debby's.

"But your hair's lovely, Claire," mum always says.

"Why is it so straight then? It's mousey and horrible and it never stays where I want it to stay."

But mum only laughs and says that I shouldn't spend so much time worrying about something that can't be changed, and that her hair is straight and mousey, too, and she enjoys looking exactly as she does. That's typical of mum. She always seems to be happy and doesn't even mind too much when the boys make a mess, or things go wrong, so it's no use going to her for sympathy because she doesn't understand what it's like to have a friend who looks like Debby.

Anyway, I'm not sure now whether I still want Debby to be my friend. I'd taken her home to have tea with us. I often do on Mondays, but this time there was only Mike there because the other two boys had stayed on for a football practice or something. Mum was busy in the kitchen so she'd laid out tea for the three of us - just Mike, Debby and myself. I suppose I hadn't noticed before that Debby never sits next to Mike when my other brothers are there, nor does she ever speak to him. This time though she kept looking at me all the time, chattering away about things we'd done at school that day and about the new shoes she was going to get, without even looking at Mike once. I'm sure he must have noticed because, after a bit, he said he wasn't hungry and he went upstairs to his room. I couldn't think why Debby was so strange, but I was surprised when she said she didn't want to stay afterwards as she'd promised her mum she wouldn't be late.

"What's wrong?" I said. "I thought you liked coming here. You always have before."

I thought she wasn't going to answer but then she stood up and said, "Yes, I do. Only I don't know what to say to your brother. Has he always been like that?"

Then I understood! I was so angry that Debby could have said such a thing when I thought she was my friend. I suppose I never notice Mike's scar any more and I forget that other people still do. He had something wrong with his mouth when he was born and mum said that the doctors had been very clever in making everything all right again, but the scar that was left was always going to be a part of Mike's face. I suppose you couldn't blame Debby for only seeing the scar and not really looking at Mike himself.

Once I stopped being angry, I felt quite sorry for Debby. It can't be much fun living in that big house with only photographs of yourself to look at. I'm so lucky having someone like Mike to live with. He told me once that I was the best sister in the world. He's always been good at saying nice things like that. He's also brilliant at ice-skating and swimming as well as running, which, it seems to me, makes him the best brother in the world.

PRAYER:

Help me try not to judge people only from the way they look.

Uncle Jack

Dean Barlow is always boasting about his Uncle Jack. He makes his uncle sound as if he should be in the Guinness Book of Records. He seems to do everything better than anyone else and has the most amazing adventures which always seem to end with Uncle Jack proving how brilliant he is, and how stupid other people are.

I do like listening to Dean, although every time I hear his stories they do make me dislike his uncle more and more!

Last Monday morning, for instance, I knew I must be missing something when I saw a crowd of boys standing around Dean in the playground, so I rushed across to find out what was going on.

Dean didn't even notice me. "So there he was," he said, "with this mad dog hanging on to his ankle, while he was fighting back the flames and helping the old lady to get down from her balcony, all at the same time."

"Then your uncle must have rabies by now," said Trevor Johnson, who doesn't have much time for Dean.

Dean looked puzzled. "What's rabies?" he said.

"You get it from mad dogs," Trevor said. "My dad knew someone who went to Spain and stroked a dog and it bit him, and he had to have injections."

"I didn't say it bit Uncle Jack," said Dean. "Anyway, do you want to hear the end or not?"

The boys pushed closer, "Yeah . . . Shut up, Trev. Go on, Dean."

"Well it might be in the paper soon," said Dean, "because one of the firemen told my uncle afterwards that he was a hero and deserves a medal."

"But what did he actually do?" I said.

Dean looked surprised and said, "Oh hi, I didn't know you were there. I was just saying that Uncle Jack saved an old lady from a fire on Saturday night. He had to break two windows and a door, but he got her out even when he was being attacked by a huge dog! The lady is so well off, I bet she's going to leave Uncle Jack all her money when she dies."

Then the bell went, so I didn't have time to ask Dean any more, and when I got out of school that afternoon, he shot off without me.

Mum had asked me to call at the supermarket on my way home as she needed some eggs and a bag of sugar. It was quite busy and I had a long wait at the checkout. There was a man there sorting out the trolleys and he kept looking at me.

Then he suddenly spoke. "You're Steve, aren't you? I've seen you with Dean. He's always talking about you. I'm his Uncle Jack," he grinned. "I thought he might have mentioned me, because I'm living with them at the moment, with Dean and his mum."

I stared at him. "You're Uncle Jack?"

"Dean's mum is my sister. Funny that Dean's never mentioned me."

"Oh, but he has," I said. "He's always talking about you. He told us about when you drove across Australia on your own and your car broke down and you had no water. And about when you rescued a climber from Snowdon, and about Saturday, with the mad dog and the fire and everything."

"Mad dog? Fire? I was gardening all weekend!" he said. Then he smiled.

He had a nice, friendly, ordinary sort of face, and I wanted to go on talking, but when someone came and told him to move the trolleys he just said, "I'll have to have a word with Dean, I can see that."

And that was that. I don't think I shall tell Dean that I've met his uncle, at least not yet. I rather like his stories, and after all, you can't make up many interesting stories about someone who pushes trolleys about in a supermarket, can you?

I did tell Mum though, and she says it's perhaps because Dean's dad died when he was a baby, and that when you've only got one uncle, you might want people to realise how very special he is.

PRAYER:

Help me always to tell the truth but also to understand why sometimes people pretend that things are more exciting than they really are.

Crying Wolf

Ann met Beverley at a birthday party and they stayed together all through the games until the very end. At first, Ann was feeling very alone, as she didn't know many of the girls there. She didn't even know Jane very well who had sent her the invitation, so she was pleased when Beverley came to sit down with her.

"There's going to be a conjuror," Beverley announced. "Let's go over there so we can see him properly."

Ann could see straight away that Beverley was the sort of person who would always know what was happening as well as the best place to sit. Ann had never found conjuring tricks very interesting, because however clever they were, they always made her feel as if she'd been cheated somehow. So it was nice to have someone like Beverley as a new friend who made everything seem more exciting.

One day, when Ann was sitting in Beverley's garden, waiting for her to bring out some lemonade, she heard a sudden scream and saw Beverley rushing across the lawn, clutching a bloodstained cloth.

"The knife slipped!" she said. "I was trying to cut up a lemon and I can't stop the bleeding! I think I've cut my finger off!"

Ann knew that there was no one in the house, and, seeing how terrified her friend was, she realised that she was the only one who could help. The sight of all the blood made her want to run away, but with her heart thumping, she said, "Let me see. We'll tie the cloth very tight and then I'll ring for an ambulance."

But before she could touch the cloth, she saw that Beverley was beginning to laugh.

"Caught you!" she said. "You should have seen your face! Look, it's just a joke thumb. And this is only red paint!"

She went on laughing, but Ann's legs felt suddenly shaky. "I don't think I'll stop for the lemonade now," she said.

"Can't you take a joke?" Beverley laughed and she was still laughing at school the next day. On another day, Beverley caught Ann out again by playing another trick. So gradually, Ann learned not to believe her any more, but they went on being friends just as before.

There were lots of things to enjoy together like the next school trip. It was to be a day trip, and they were both excited at the thought of climbing some hills, and visiting an outdoor centre where they were to meet a real Mountain Rescue team.

When the day finally came, they couldn't wait to set off into the hills even though it was raining. The teachers organised everybody into small groups, each with an adult, and they began their climb, following a steep winding track until the coach they had travelled in looked like a small brown dot far below.

For a time, Beverley and Ann stayed close, but gradually Beverley moved on to join the group ahead, and after ten minutes, Ann lost sight of her. The rain was heavy again now, and Ann was too breathless to talk to anyone, so, for the next hour she didn't mind too much about Beverley leaving her.

Then suddenly she heard shouting, and saw someone running back down the hill towards her. "Beverley Johnson's been hurt. She wandered off on her own and fell from a rock.They think she's broken her ankle so we'll need a stretcher."

"There's no need," Ann said. "Beverley's always playing tricks like this. I thought she was planning something. It's only another of her jokes."

The teacher with the group looked shocked. "Ann - that's an awful thing to say! She wouldn't pretend anything like this. Anyway, we're all going back to the coach to wait there. The Rescue people are in charge now."

The teacher was right, Beverley really had fallen. She had hurt her ankle, and they all had to wait until she was ready to go home with her foot in plaster. Most people would have grumbled about the pain, but Beverley made a joke about it, which made Ann feel even more ashamed for not believing her.

They're still good friends, but Ann has noticed that Beverley has stopped buying things from the joke shop now. Ann is very pleased about that, of course, but sometimes she still wonders what would have happened to Beverley on that hillside if everyone else had believed it was only a joke.

PRAYER:

Help me to remember that if I make people believe that something is true when it isn't, then I cannot expect them to believe me when I am speaking the truth.

Listen to Me

In the school holidays, mum and I always go swimming on Wednesdays. I thought my new friend Gemma might like to come with us, although she always goes to her gran's on Wednesday afternoons. I knew Gemma loved swimming so we asked her the next week, but she said, "Why don't you come with me to gran's instead?"

When I told mum about the invitation she said, "Why don't you go? I've been wanting to go to the hairdresser's for ages and this would be a good chance."

Gemma seemed really pleased when I said I'd like to go with her.

"Gran's got her own little flat," she told me. "But she doesn't know anybody around here, and she can't even walk to the park any more. We all try and go on a different day of the week so that she has lots of visitors, and then she comes to us every Sunday. I hope you're hungry because she always bakes on Wednesday mornings and makes all the things that I like."

It was quite a long walk, but soon after we'd passed the station, we came to a small block of new flats. Gemma had to press a button at the door and speak to her gran before the door opened into a long hall. It smelt of new paint, and there were two wheelchairs at the end of the hall, animal pictures on the walls and lots of bowls of flowers.

"Gran has had to learn to be tidy here," said Gemma, giggling. "You should have seen her old house. She reads masses of books and they used to be all over the floor, and there were always people coming and going because she had so many friends."

By now I was feeling quite sorry for her gran, because I'm not very tidy either, but then I saw that one of the doors was open.

"Here we are," said Gemma, and she led me into a room where there was a very old lady sitting by the window.

"This is Caroline," Gemma said, and then she did something very strange with her hands and fingers. The old lady smiled and said, "Hello, Caroline," but then she began to move her fingers as well. Gemma laughed, and then said to me, "She says she's made some meringues as well as some chocolate cake. She likes me to read as well as to sign." Then she turned again, and watched the old lady's fingers. "Some flapjack too . . . come on, let's go and talk to Rupert."

Rupert was a large black cat, and he purred very loudly when I stroked him.

"Do you like cats, Caroline?" the old lady asked.

"Yes, I do! I wish we had one."

I watched as Gemma made some more strange signs and then watched the old lady again.

"Rupert seems to like you," she said, making a movement that made me think of someone pouring some tea, then she went into the kitchen.

Gemma smiled and said, "Gran's been deaf since she was small. My grandpa was partly deaf too. So we've all learnt to use another language."

"Another language?" I said. "But you weren't speaking."

"It's still a language" Gemma said. "It's called the British Sign Language. It took me a long time to learn, although some of the signs anyone can understand. I could teach you some, if you like. Hand shapes are the easiest. Look, this is a house, and this is a table, and this is a mat . . . "

I interrupted her. "I couldn't remember all that. And you go far too quickly."

The tea we had together was one of the most interesting meals I had ever had. Afterwards, I tried to explain to my mum how I had not felt left out at all. We'd all laughed at so many things together. I felt I almost understood what Gemma was signing because I watched her eyes and face as well. It made me want to use my own hands and fingers to talk to the old lady - and, of course, I ate so much that Gemma said, "Gran will have to bake even more next time you come!"

And I know that even though I like swimming, I'll certainly want to go to tea at gran's again, if only to watch my friend speaking another language, and to try to learn a little of it myself. Not that I need to try it out on Rupert. He can hear even the smallest squeak of a mouse!

PRAYER:

Help me to realise how much we depend on our sight and our hearing and to understand how difficult life becomes without them.

Wishing

I always know when Sharon is in a bad mood. She slams her bedroom door and she won't come out, not even when mum calls her. My brother, Terry, often makes it worse by banging on the door, asking if she's taken one of his cassettes. He keeps them in a box under his bed - I'm sure he checks them every night - he always seems to know as soon as one is missing. It's not always Sharon's fault when he's lost one but sometimes it's because she's always borrowing things without asking.

My name's Chloe and sometimes I wish I didn't have a sister, at least not one like Sharon. She's older than Terry and I but not as old as Jack who's nearly sixteen and taller than dad. I don't mind too much about her being bossy, but I wish she didn't always want the things that other people have.

I always know there's going to be trouble when someone at school has some new shoes or goes on holiday somewhere exciting. Sharon starts pestering mum, and when she's told we can't afford things like that, Sharon always flounces off upstairs and slams her bedroom door. I don't know why she thinks it's going to make any difference, because eventually she has to come downstairs and start talking to us again. We all try and pretend that nothing has happened, but we know it's going to happen again because Sharon is . . . well . . . she's just Sharon, who's always wishing for things she hasn't got.

Anyway, when she heard that Pippa Barlow was having some private lessons at a drama school in town, she told mum, and we had several nights of slammed bedroom doors and arguments.

"Pippa says she might be asked to be in the pantomime at the Theatre Royal next year, and it's only because she's having lessons. She might be on television too."

Mum, who was busy peeling some potatoes, sighed and said, "Since when did you get this idea? You always hated being in the Christmas plays at your last school."

"And once you forgot your lines," I said, "when you had to say, 'The star has brought us safely to this stable'. Even I could have remembered that."

"That was only kids' stuff," Sharon said. "I'm talking about real acting."

"Apart from the cost of private lessons, you've enough to do with all your exams," mum said.

They went on arguing for ages after that, until at last Sharon went up to her room and slammed the door again.

I don't really know Pippa Barlow very well. She has her hair in spikes and two gold rings in her eyebrow. She looks like a lot of the girls at Sharon's new school who all dress the same and look like models you see in magazines. So I was surprised when I met her at the end of our road one day last week. She wasn't with Sharon, who had already got back from school, and it surprised me when Pippa stepped out from a gateway and said, "It's Chloe, isn't it? Sharon's sister?"

"She's at home if you want her," I said.

Pippa shook her head. "No, I just wondered if your brother was around."

"Terry? He's gone to the allotment with dad."

"I meant Jack." I saw that Pippa's face had gone quite red. "I could ring him if I had his number," she said. "I just wish he'd notice me. I think he's so dishy."

"Dad won't let him have a mobile phone yet," I said. "Sorry!"

I ran off down the road before she had time to ask me anything else. I giggled at the thought of someone like Pippa wanting to get to know my brother. I didn't tell mum, but I did say something to Sharon.

"Your friend Pippa doesn't always get what she wants," I said, "even if she does go to drama classes."

"What do you mean?" she said.

"You'll have to ask Pippa." I didn't say another word.

I think I'm rather pleased now that I have a big brother like Jack who doesn't even like girls with gold rings in their eyebrows. Somehow I don't think Sharon's wish is going to come true this time.

PRAYER:

Help me not to be envious of other people if they seem to be luckier than I am and to enjoy my own life exactly as it is.

A Picnic with Grandpa

Grandpa always wants to go on picnics. He doesn't seem to mind if it's raining or even if there's snow on the ground.

"You must make sure you get lots of fresh air," he always says. "Whatever the weather."

When Martin and I are standing with our sandwiches and shivering with the cold, he'll say, "Put your shoulders back and take a deep breath. That's it. Fill up your lungs."

Grandpa is always telling us what we ought to do. Most of the time we don't really mind because he makes up smashing games and is much better at pretending things than mum and dad are. I remember once when they were both out, grandpa put off all the lights and took us through every room of the house, pretending that we came from the future and that we were looking at a place where people used to live hundreds of years ago.

"Here's my torch, Sally," he said. "Now you can be the guide, and you've got to explain everything you see, pretending that you've never seen it before, like that ladder over there."

"Those are the stairs, grandpa, not a ladder."

"But we don't know that, do we? Because we're from the future and we know how to elevate ourselves without using wooden steps called stairs."

We liked that game, and the torch made everything more exciting; it didn't look like our house at all. Mum would never have thought of a game like that, and when she came home that night she started telling us that it was dangerous to play in the dark and that she'd nearly tripped over my shoes in the hall, and that I always ought to put them somewhere out of the way.

Martin and I have decided that adults must like giving advice because they do it so often and never miss a chance of telling you what you should do and how you ought do it. That's exactly what grandpa was doing on a picnic one day last summer.

For once, it was a lovely sunny day and we went down by the river to my favourite place. Mum had packed some cheese sandwiches; there were some apples and grapes for afters, as well as a banana each.

Before we started eating, grandpa said, "Now do watch out for wasps and don't put anything into your mouth before you check it first."

When anyone gives you advice you try and remember at first, but you soon forget again, and there were so many things to look at that day that even grandpa must have forgotten too. I suppose you could say it was my fault really, only I'd seen this flash of blue across by the bushes on the other side of the river.

"Look - there's a Kingfisher!"

We'd only ever seen one once before so it was really exciting. Martin saw it, too, and so did grandpa, but only for a brief moment because it darted out of sight straight away. Martin scrambled down the bank to get a better view, and even grandpa stood up and was pointing over the river with his banana.

"There he goes again!" he said, and he put his banana in his mouth. Then he gave a shout and clutched at his mouth.

"I've been stung!" he yelled, and he cupped his hands and spat out the wasp that had settled on the banana. That was the end of the picnic, and we called in at the chemist on the way home to check that grandpa didn't need to see the doctor. The chemist said he'd been lucky because the wasp hadn't stung grandpa's throat and that the swelling on his lip would soon go down.

All the way back, neither Martin nor I said a word about how grandpa had done exactly what he had told us not to do. We tried not to laugh when we remembered how he had waved his banana into the air like a pointer. Grandpa must have known what we were thinking because when we got home he suddenly said, "It was worth being stung to see your lovely Kingfisher, Sally. I'm glad you spotted it." And he didn't even say a word about hanging up our coats or going to wash our hands as he generally did, so I wasn't really surprised when I heard Martin say, "When can we go on another picnic, grandpa?" because that was just what I was going to say.

PRAYER:

Nobody likes being told what to do but help me to realise that people often give advice only because they care about our safety and well-being.

Just Among Friends

Lucy's birthday was on the 24th December. If she could have chosen another date it would have been a summer one like Sue's whose birthday was in July, which seemed a much better idea.

Her Aunt Polly used to say the same thing every year. "Happy Birthday, Lucy. I think that this time it will have to be a combined birthday and Christmas present, if you don't mind." Lucy generally managed to say that it didn't matter at all and that she quite understood - but it did seem unfair.

Dad even pretended that it was only because it was Christmas Eve that he could remember Lucy's birthday. Lucy thought he was just saying that to make her laugh, but actually dad did forget a lot of things, and once he had completely forgotten mum's birthday.

Mum didn't live with them any more so Lucy could see that dad had a lot to do what with the shopping, the cooking and all the washing. Anyway, he often did make her laugh and Sue said she wished her father would make jokes too.

Sue and Lucy had been friends for a long time. They never seemed to have enough time to talk about all the things they wanted to, but things changed when Alison moved into their class. She started waiting for them after school and seemed really anxious to get to know them. She was always giving them packets of crisps or chocolate bars, and telling them how her dad could get them free tickets for any film they wanted to see. Once or twice Alison and Sue went off together on their own, and Lucy began to feel that Sue was no longer her special friend.

Still, you couldn't help liking Alison. Even dad said he didn't mind if they went to her party so long as they weren't too late coming home.

"At least she's planned her birthday for the summer when it's light in the evenings," he said and laughed as if Lucy had chosen a December birthday just to be difficult, but when Lucy and Sue got to the party, Alison was nowhere to be seen.

Neither of them had been to Alison's house before, but they'd written down her address carefully and found out that it was only a few streets away from where Lucy's Aunt Polly lived.

There were lots of girls already there, and one of them, a girl called Donna, asked them why they had come because it was her party and had nothing to do with Alison at all.

"But Alison asked us to come and she gave us this address," said Lucy.

Everybody laughed and stared at Lucy and Sue, who by this time felt really stupid, still clutching their presents for Alison and not knowing what to do.

Then one of the girls watching pushed forward and said, "She's done this before to someone I know. She pretends that you didn't write the address down properly, so that it's your fault that you've come to the wrong party. When you see her next time, she'll tell you all about her own party and how great it was."

"But why?" said Lucy. "Why does she do that?"

The girl shrugged. "It makes her feel good, I suppose, and she'll go on saying that you're her friends, pretending that she has parties like everybody else, but she never does."

People were still staring so Lucy said, "Let's go and see Aunt Polly instead of going straight home." So they did, and Aunt Polly made some lovely lemonade and they sat in her garden and ate strawberries while they talked about Alison.

"I don't think I like pretend friends," said Lucy as they set off for home. "Real friends never make you feel stupid, do they?"

"Never," said Sue, and she handed her the small parcel she had taken to the party. "Here you are. We can count this visit to Aunt Polly's as your first summer birthday party!"

Lucy didn't know why she was so surprised. After all, she thought happily . . . it was just what any real friend would do to make someone feel better.

PRAYER:

Help me to realise who my real friends are and to appreciate how lucky I am to know them.

Playing a Part

"This year," said Miss Richards, "our play is going to be about someone called Rumpelstiltskin, and there'll be plenty of parts for everybody." She smiled at the class, and Liz felt sure that the smile was meant mostly for her. After all, everybody had said how good she had been in the last play when she'd played Cinderella, and Miss Richards had said that she wished everybody could have learned their lines as well as Liz had.

Liz turned around to look at her friend, Rachel, who always has a place near the window, as she can't read anything unless it's in very large print. Rachel had been very good in Cinderella too, though she played an Ugly Sister and had made everybody laugh.

Later, Miss Richards gave out the copies of the script and said that, as there weren't too many speaking parts, she'd choose the final cast after she'd heard everyone read the parts they would each like to play. Liz knew straight away that she wanted to play the part of Marigold, the daughter of a poor miller, who in the end marries the King because she learns how to turn straw into gold. She was surprised when Rachel came to her in the playground and said, "I'd like to be the miller's daughter. Rumpelstiltskin tells her the secret about turning straw into gold and . . ."

Liz interrupted her. "I know all that," she said, angrily, "but I thought you liked funny parts."

Rachel looked shocked. "Not always," she said. "Anyway, I've told Miss Richards that I'd like to do it."

For the next few days Liz never told Rachel that she too, was going to read the part of the miller's daughter, and even when Rachel asked her which part she liked best, Liz pretended that she was still deciding whether to be a courtier or a villager, or one of the people who tried to guess the name of Rumpelstiltskin. The following morning everyone went up on to the stage to read the parts they wanted to do. Liz did her reading first and then two other girls, and finally Rachel. Miss Richards listened carefully then smiled and thanked everybody, but it wasn't until the next day that she read out the names of the ones she had chosen.

Liz could hardly believe her ears! Rachel was to be the miller's daughter, the biggest part in the whole play, while she was to be one of the villagers who had to make up ridiculous names until at last somebody guessed the right name for Rumpelstiltskin. Fighting back the tears of disappointment, Liz dashed out of the hall, aware only of the awful pain of knowing that she had been rejected in front of all her friends. Somehow she managed to get through the day, but as she was putting on her jacket to go home, she felt a touch on her arm and saw that Rachel was holding out a copy of the script.

"You left this in the hall this morning," she said. "I've been looking for you all day. Is something wrong?"

Liz gulped, "No," and she ran off without even looking at Rachel.

That night when she was going to bed, she told her mother the whole story.

"I feel awful now, mum," she said. "I wanted that part so much. I was so angry with Rachel and with Miss Richards for choosing her. I was horrible to Rachel."

Mum was silent for a moment and then she said, "Last year, Rachel's mum told me that the one part Rachel was hoping for was Cinderella."

"Cinderella? But I never knew. She never said anything, and she told me I was really good and that it was fun being an Ugly Sister and making people laugh."

"That's just like Rachel," mum said. "She's very good when it comes to pretending things. So are you. I have a feeling that once you try and pretend you don't mind too much about all this, you might suddenly find that you don't. It won't be easy, but why don't you try?"

Liz didn't believe her for a moment, but when the phone rang and she heard Rachel's voice asking if she was all right, she knew that there could only be one answer.

"I'm fine," she said. "I was just telling mum how good you're going to be as the miller's daughter."

After all, as mum had said, she was quite good at pretending, and it didn't really hurt all that much.

PRAYER:

*Help me to learn to accept disappointments as cheerfully as
I can.*

The Outsider

I knew mum was expecting visitors. I was supposed to come home straight from school, but I'd forgotten about it, until my friend Karen reminded me. Karen's much better than I am at remembering things. I could hear people laughing as I came up to the front door, and mum called out straight away. "We're in the diner, Sara," she said, in that funny voice she often uses when we have visitors.

For once I remembered to hang up my coat and schoolbag before I went in to meet them. Mum was wearing her new dress and the twins were still in clean t-shirts, which meant they hadn't had their tea yet. Anyway, I saw that we had two visitors, a Mrs Williams and a girl about my own age.

"This is my daughter, Sara," mum said, as if we were at Buckingham Palace or somewhere. "This is Mrs Williams and Jodie, Sara. I think you two are going to be great friends."

I'd never met anyone called Jodie before and at first I quite liked her . . . but I soon changed my mind. Once she'd started talking she never stopped, and all through tea she went on and on telling us about how she once had a pony and what a big house they had in Bristol.

Mrs Williams didn't try to stop her like mum would have done if I'd talked non-stop all through tea, but I was surprised when she said, "Jodie is starting at your school next Monday, Sara. She won't know anyone, but your mother says you'll stay with her while she settles in."

I glared at mum who was busy pouring the tea, so I had to wait until the visitors had gone.

"Why did you say that?" I said. "Nobody will like her and I shall be stuck with her all the time."

When we got to school the following Monday, things were even worse than I had expected. Firstly, Mrs Williams brought her around to our house so that we had to get the school bus together, and I couldn't sit with Karen as I usually do. Then Jodie began talking just as she'd done in the kitchen, and when one of the boys started laughing, she told him he was stupid and that she hated boys with spots.

Then everybody ganged up against her, and by the time we got off the bus, we'd been left all on our own. I tried to explain to Karen about not sitting with her, but she just ran off, and I was left with Jodie. Mum had told me to take her into the school office first. I hoped I could leave her there, but they told her we'd be in the same class and I had to show her where everything was. I really was stuck with her.

Someone else had taken my place at dinnertime so I couldn't sit with Karen, and when a girl accidentally knocked against Jodie's chair, she almost started a fight, saying that she'd done it on purpose.

Everybody hated her. I wanted to say, "Look, I'm not really with her. It's not my fault," but I knew I couldn't, at least not on her first day.

Since then I've often felt like telling her she'll never make any friends if she goes on thinking she's better than everybody else, but I'm glad now that I didn't. Last week mum told me something I didn't know before. She said that Jodie's father had worked in a bank, but they'd found out that he'd been taking money from someone else's account and now he was in prison, and that's why Mrs Williams had wanted to move somewhere new.

"I think there's going to be a divorce," mum said. "Jodie might not be able to see her father very much, even when he comes out of prison. Poor Jodie. At least she's had you to help her get used to her new life."

Jodie still hangs around with me all the time, but maybe I'm getting used to her a bit more now, or perhaps she's changing too. Yesterday, she even sat with Kay Johnson on the school bus and I heard them laughing and talking non-stop the whole way there. I hope she does start to make her own friends soon because you can't look after someone forever, especially if you don't like them very much.

PRAYER:

It isn't easy to like every person we meet, but help me to remember how it feels when we have to meet a lot of strangers.

The Grumblers

The notice on the end garage was in very big letters. It read, NO BALL GAMES, only the paint had faded a lot and it had lost its letter 'S'. The garages were built around a large empty space, which was far wider than the road where Sean and Pete lived and much better for kicking balls around than anywhere else they knew.

The problem was that old Mr Bagshaw lived in a big stone house beyond the garages, and he was always coming out to shout at them when they played there. Sometimes, Miss Woodcroft, who lived at No.13, would come out and say that they were making far too much noise and would they all go away, and play somewhere else?

Dave, who was another friend of theirs, never got cross when Miss Woodcroft sent them packing or when old Mr Bagshaw started waving his stick, because he knew Sean and Pete would do all the grumbling for him. In fact, if he ever tried to cheer them up, he'd find that they would turn on him instead, so he'd long since decided that they just enjoyed grumbling and would never change.

One day, when they were really fed up about having nowhere to play, they suddenly saw Miss Woodcroft opening the door of one of the garages.

"I didn't know she had a car," Sean said.

Dave suddenly remembered something his mother had said only that morning.

"It's a new one," he said. "She's never had one before and she didn't want to leave it in the street in case it gets wet." The boys were still laughing when they suddenly heard a shout and saw Mr Bagshaw sprawled out on his front steps. Miss Woodcroft saw him too, and she left the garage and called to the boys to help.

Together they managed to get the old man back on to his feet. He seemed confused, but they eventually got him into the house again and settled into an armchair.

"I think he's all right," Miss Woodcroft said. "I'll drive to the surgery and ask if someone could come to check. Do you think you could stop with him for a while? I shan't be long."

At first the boys didn't know what to say to Mr Bagshaw. He was very quiet, and he kept saying that he'd only banged his knee and that they'd no right to fetch the doctor. The house felt cold, and Dave went to the window to pull back the curtains because the room was so dark.

"Look at this!" he called to Sean. "I didn't know there was all this lawn at the back."

The boys stared, and Mr Bagshaw said, "It's a right old mess out there. I can't cope with it these days."

For once Sean was quiet too, but he did ask Mr Bagshaw if he could look at some railway books he saw on the shelf, and the old man seemed really pleased. He soon got very angry again when Miss Woodcroft came back with the district nurse.

Then the boys had to go home, but the next day they made sure they were near Miss Woodcroft's garage when she came home.

"Is he all right?" Dave asked.

Miss Woodcroft smiled. "He grumbled at me for fetching the nurse, but I think he was really frightened when he fell. Anyway, I told him how dangerous it was for you to play in the road and I asked him about that big lawn of his at the back. Nobody ever uses it and he says he can't cope with a mower any more. So I suggested that he might let you use it."

"I bet old misery guts said no," said Sean.

"Yes he did at first," said Miss Woodcroft, "until I suggested that you could keep the grass cut in return for letting you use it for your games."

And that's how it's been ever since. Sean grumbles when it's his turn to push the mower, of course, but he's just as chuffed as Dave and Pete are to have a pitch of their own. Mr Bagshaw doesn't seem to mind if they bring other boys in too, although he still grumbles a bit when he sees them all on his lawn, but as Miss Woodcroft says, you can't expect a leopard to change its spots completely.

PRAYER:

It's very easy to grumble about things we don't like but
help me to remember that I can sometimes change them.

The Rainbow

Charlotte loved Friday afternoons; that was when they did drawing and painting. Some of the class were really good and the best paintings were put up on the wall and stayed there all through the next week. There was generally one of Charlotte's up there but none of Nicola's or Jane's. They were her best friends and they liked to sit together at the same table. Jane's mum was always coming up to the school because she thought Jane wasn't working hard enough. Charlotte knew that this wasn't true because Jane tried really hard at everything, but if the class was painting a tree or a windmill, you could never tell which one Jane was trying to do. At least with Nicola's you could make a guess, but Nicola always said she couldn't really be bothered with trying to make branches look like branches, so you couldn't expect hers to be put up on the wall either -and they never were.

One wet Friday afternoon, Miss Francis, their teacher, said she wanted the whole class to paint rainbows so they would all forget about the rain outside and she said that every single painting would be put on the wall. Nicola started her rainbow right away. Even Jane said she'd have a go, but Charlotte sat back for a moment to decide where she would put her rainbow on the paper, and how she would get just the right sort of curve.

Perhaps, she thought, she would put it by a lake and then she would have two rainbows to paint, because one would be reflected in the water. Her two friends were already busy, but she leaned forward, guarding her paper, so that they would not be able to see her beautiful double rainbow.

It was difficult to get the second rainbow to look exactly like the first, but as she worked on, she became more and more pleased with the picture, and it slowly grew to cover the whole page. Beyond the lake, she painted two hills, a forest and a waterfall. Then in the meadow in front of the lake, wild flowers and two butterflies, and a small cottage with smoke rising from the chimney. She glanced around. Nicola had leaned over and was giggling at Jane's painting.

"Your rainbow is all squashed," she said.

Jane reached across and snatched at Nicola's painting. "And yours is all. . . " and then she gave a cry of horror as she sent Charlotte's pot of water flying.

"Now look what you've done!" said Charlotte. The spreading water had drenched the whole painting, and the colours blurred together as they spread over the hills and the lake, the two rainbows and the cottage. Even the wild flowers became a patch of blue, and the butterflies disappeared.

"Oh Charlotte - I'm so sorry." Jane was nearly in tears.

Miss Francis came to their table and said cheerfully, "Never mind. Accidents will happen - you'd better start again, Charlotte. Even if you don't finish, yours can go up on the wall as well."

Charlotte didn't finish a new rainbow. She didn't even try. She knew that she would never again be able to paint such a perfect one. So for the first time ever, Jane and Nicola's paintings were put up on the wall. Then Charlotte saw that Miss Francis was pinning up another painting. It was one of her own, a kingfisher Charlotte had painted during the last term.

"How's that?" Miss Francis said.

"The colours match all the rainbows," said Jane.

"It's perfect," said Nicola.

Charlotte looked at her two friends. How could she have been so angry with them both, her best friends? Already she was beginning to feel better. Miss Francis was smiling too. "Now we can all forget the rain outside," she said.

But they already had.

Prayer:

Sometimes things happen that upset us, but once they have happened, help us not to let our angry feelings spoil everything else.

Albert and Friends

It was a very hot day, even hotter than the day before, and Albert was very tired.

Albert lived in a forest among tall trees at the foot of a mountain. Sometimes the leaves of the trees above his head were so thick that they stopped the rays of the sun reaching down to the ground. But this year the sun had been shining for so long that all the leaves had shrivelled in the heat, and instead of the forest path being cool and shady, its soil was baked so hard that Albert's tiny feet were beginning to hurt.

Like all other ants in the world, Albert had to do a lot of walking, and he was very good at it. He knew he was good because he had all the other ants in his nest to compare himself with, and although he was a very modest ant, and would never have dreamed of boasting, he felt he was well above the mid-distance class of ant.

Being both a truthful and a modest ant, he was also the first to admit that his sense of direction was not quite up to the required standard. He could carry any leaf or twig to any part of the forest without the slightest difficulty, carefully following the ant in front, and never losing his place and confusing the ant who was following behind. No one, in fact, could ever have accused him of not playing his part or pulling his weight - or indeed, of carrying it - to wherever it was needed.

Today in the burning heat of the sun, it really was very hard work. The leader ant was keeping up quite a fast pace and if you'd have been sitting up in one of the trees, you would have seen a whole brownish, reddish, stream of ants flowing along the path at almost the speed of light. At least that's what it felt like to Albert.

"I wish we could slow down a bit," he puffed, lifting his twig a little higher above his head. "If I don't stop soon, I shall have one of my dizzy turns."

Hardly had he spoken the words than the trees seemed to turn upside down and his whole world turned over in a whirl of spinning branches and dazzling light.

"Goodness me!" he said. "What's happening?"

Almost immediately his head stopped its circling, and he realised that he had dropped his twig. But there was no sign of it on the ground. All he could see were the huge leaves of a strange plant. The path had disappeared and so had all the other ants. Then he realised the awful truth. In his moment of dizziness, he had left the path and was now completely lost.

Worse than that, he'd forgotten where he was supposed to be going. He felt he would never be able to overcome the shame of it. He knew just how important it was that each ant could be relied upon to carry out the work required by the family nest. He remembered that he had been carrying a twig, so somehow he had to find it again and get back to the path - wherever it was. But even though he searched and searched, and climbed up stems and over leaves, there seemed to be no sign of it.

Suddenly he saw a much bigger twig, broken off from a tree that must have died a long time before. It was much heavier than his own twig, and it had an awkward bend in its middle, but at last he managed to balance it, and weaving his way through the plants, he set off again to look for the path.

When nearly all his strength had gone, his feet at last reached some smooth, sun-baked soil, but by then he was exhausted. The path still looked unfamiliar, and already the forest was darkening and showing the beginning of the night. There was no way he could survive on his own. In a final panic, he tried to go faster, until he suddenly saw that the path was widening, and that ahead of him, was a familiar leader ant from his own nest. And he was not alone, for behind him were all Albert's friends, returning home to the nest.

Most of them were carrying seeds and grain now, and seeing a small gap, he fitted himself quickly into the line of workers as if he had never left it. Although his twig was just as heavy and he knew there was a long way to go, never before had Albert felt so happy. No longer alone, he felt the strength and energy of all the ants around him surge into his own legs, as the long line moved swiftly and silently through the blackness towards the safety of their own nest.

DISCUSSION TOPIC:

Recognising the importance of friends and of the value of everything familiar to us.

Too Many Birthdays

"The trouble with me is that I've had too many birthdays." That was what gran was always saying.

Denise and Paula didn't know how many birthdays she'd actually had because whenever they asked her how old she was she'd say, "As old as my tongue and a little older than my teeth."

Mum generally interrupted at that point, telling them to go and tidy their rooms or something and not to pester gran. The girls loved having her stay. Sometimes, when they were in bed, she'd come upstairs and, if she was in a good mood, she'd tell them lovely adventure stories about a girl who could climb mountains, and ride horses, and race through rapids in a canoe, and who once swam across a lake to escape from a bear.

They liked the story of the bear and would always ask her the same questions.

"Was it a real bear, gran?"

"Well, of course it was. It had been coming into the town to look for food and people were warned to be on their guard wherever they went."

Usually, once she'd finished telling them the stories, gran would say she wanted to watch something on television, and they wouldn't see her again until the morning, but on this particular visit, she said something else.

"Your father helped me to clear out my attic before we came here today," she said, "so tomorrow night we shan't be watching television. I've got a surprise for you."

They tried to persuade her to tell them what the surprise was going to be, but gran just stood up and told them they'd have to wait and see. It always takes her a long time to stand up when she's been sitting down, and this time it was a real struggle after sitting on Paula's bed.

"I'm glad I'm not old," Denise said, after gran had gone downstairs. "And I'd hate to keep forgetting things. She's always losing her glasses."

"I'd never fall asleep in front of the television like she does."

But they forgot all those things when, on the next evening, they found a big screen put up in front of the television. Dad was fiddling with an old projector that he'd brought from gran's attic, and mum had put some chairs in a row as if it was a cinema.

"You won't have seen this film before," said gran. "In fact it must be twenty years since I saw it myself."

The film was a bit blurred, and someone had written "Vancouver Island" at the beginning. It all seemed to be about a girl. Sometimes she was climbing, and sometimes she was in a little canoe on a river with rocks and white foam. She kept waving to the camera, and once she began dancing, and then standing on her hands. Then they saw her swimming in a lake, and she lifted her hands and waved towards them all.

"It's a pity you can't see the bear," said gran. "But that was another time. When I'd gone for a walk without your grandpa."

Then mum put on the lights again, and they saw that gran was laughing.

"Look at your faces!" gran said. "Didn't you recognise me?"

Denise stared at her. "You mean you were that girl? But she stood on her hands!"

"I was very good at that," said gran. "And I was faster than your grandpa when it came to swimming. We had this wonderful Canadian holiday and your grandfather had got this new kind of camera. Most of the films have got lost over the years but your father found the projector yesterday morning and just this one film."

That night in bed, the girls had a lot to talk about. The girl in the film looked nothing like gran looked now, and yet somehow they could see it was her.

"Do you think she still remembers how to stand on her hands?" said Paula.

"She said she did. And I believe her, don't you?"

Paula nodded. "Yes I do. But we'd better not ask her to do it!"

PRAYER:

Help me to realise that people who are old were once just like me.

Mortimer's Move

Mortimer was not a happy rat. He loved his little home in the riverbank. It was warm and cosy but he felt it was time to move.

"The river is much too noisy," he said. "It keeps me awake all night. I must find a new home."

He stayed there for one more night, and all that night the water splashed and gurgled around the riverbank.

"It is no good," he said the next morning. "I can't stay here any longer. I shall ask my friends to help me to look for a new home."

First he went to his friend, the brown cow. "I'm looking for a new home," Mortimer said. "Will you come with me to look? Then perhaps you might find a new home too."

The brown cow looked very surprised. "But I don't want to move," she said. "The grass round here is the best I've ever tasted, so I shall stay here."

So Mortimer went on until he came to the bridge where he met his friend, the hedgehog. "I'm looking for a new home," he said. "Will you come with me to look? Then perhaps you might find a new home too."

"Sorry," said the hedgehog. "I don't want to move. This is my favourite bridge. I've crossed it three times already this morning and I've never found a better bridge anywhere, so I shall stay here."

Mortimer felt very sad, but on he went until he became so tired that he just had to sit down and have a rest. In a moment, he was fast asleep, but after a while something woke him up. He could feel it touching his whiskers.

"Goodness me!" said Mortimer, as he opened his eyes. There in front of him was a rat with a gleaming brown coat.

"I didn't mean to make you jump," she said, "but perhaps you can help me. I'm looking for a new home."

"Are you really?" said Mortimer. "That's very odd. So am I."

The brown rat looked very unhappy. "I live in the barn at the top of the hill over there," she said. "It's warm and cosy but very noisy. Up on the hill the wind is always blowing, and it keeps me awake every night."

"It's the river that keeps me awake," said Mortimer, "but I love the sound of the wind."

"And I love the sound of water," said the brown rat. "If only I had a home in the river bank."

"And if only I had a home at the top of a hill," sighed Mortimer. Then, in that moment, they both had the very same idea. Mortimer looked at the brown rat and the brown rat looked at Mortimer.

"The sound of the wind always makes me sleepy," said Mortimer. "I would sleep like a log if I lived on the top of the hill."

"And I can never keep awake when I hear the sound of water," said the brown rat. "I would sleep like a log if I lived in your home by the river."

So that night, when the moon was full, the two rats moved into their new homes. Mortimer moved into the barn on the hill, and the brown rat moved into the hole in the river bank. All through the night, the river splashed and gurgled as it always had done, and, as it always had done, the wind blew over the barn at the top of the hill.

But neither of them heard a sound because they were both fast asleep!

PRAYER:

Help me to enjoy all the differences between people.

Sorry – I Forgot!

Harvey was great at lending you things. In fact, that was the first thing that Lewis noticed about him. People were always going up to him and saying they'd lost their pens or their swimming kit or a letter they were supposed to post for their mum, and somehow Harvey would always sort it out.

The missing items were generally found somewhere in the school, so it was always Harvey that people went to. Lewis knew he was lucky when they started being friends because he often lost things too. It was always a mystery how they disappeared. His mum said it was because he never kept his mind on one thing at a time. That was probably why he lost his anorak one Monday morning.

"Leave it to me," Harvey said. "I'm going home at dinnertime. I'll bring you my spare one. It's the same colour as yours so your mum won't notice tonight. Then when yours turns up, we can do a swap again."

Lewis waited eagerly for him to come back to school that afternoon. Everything that Harvey owned seemed to be better than anyone else's, so Lewis knew that all the other boys would notice the difference. Yet Harvey never came back that day. Nor did he come to school on the following day, so Lewis found himself in deep trouble when mum saw him creeping into the hall that second night.

"You're soaked through," she said. "Where's your jacket? You said you didn't take it to school yesterday because it was too hot, but why didn't you wear it this morning? They said it was going to rain."

His dad, hearing her voice, came through from the kitchen. "Do you realise what we paid for that thing?"

Lewis looked at his father's face. His dad always seemed to be in a bad mood these days, and since he'd lost his job, he was at home every day when Lewis came home from school.

Thinking quickly, he said, "I lent it to Harvey. He'd forgotten his and he's further to go than I have."

"I would have thought that Harvey would have rung for a taxi," said dad bitterly. "That family must be rolling, living in a house like that, and with all those cars."

"They've only got two," said Lewis. "One's his mum's."

"It's two more than we've got. So mind you get it back tomorrow."

In the morning, there was no sign of Harvey in the playground, and Lewis's heart sank. He'd have to tell the truth when he got home. He hadn't even told Harvey that he'd gone into the amusement arcade in town before he'd caught the bus that Monday morning, or that he'd lost all his pocket money on one of its machines. He must have put the jacket down on the floor while he played and had forgotten it when he realised what time it was. He daren't even go back to the arcade because they would have told the school. Then he would have been in even worse trouble.

Later in the morning, when he was looking out of the window, he saw a car stop at the school gate and saw Harvey and his mother get out.

He didn't see Harvey again until dinnertime when he came into the school hall. He looked quite pale, and when he saw Lewis, he tried to turn away.

"Did you bring the spare?" said Lewis. "And where were you yesterday?"

"Mum kept me at home. I forgot all about it."

"But you promised!" Lewis said. "You said you would. How could you forget?"

"Well, I did, didn't I?" Harvey said. "So what?"

Lewis stared at Harvey. Surely this couldn't be his best friend, the one friend who never let him down? His chest hurt, as if someone had hit it hard, and he made sure he never spoke to Harvey again all that day. But at night, after he'd told his parents the whole truth, he was surprised that they seemed to be more concerned about Harvey than they were about the missing jacket.

"Poor lad," mum said. "There were police round there all day, and folk say they won't have a penny to call their own when all the debts are paid off. It can't have been easy for Harvey to find out his dad is in serious trouble."

Lewis thought of all the times Harvey had helped him before, and of all the fun they'd had together. Suddenly ashamed of how he had blamed his friend for not remembering one small promise, Lewis knew what he had to do.

"Can I go round to Harvey's straight away?" he said. "He'll need his best friend to cheer him up."

PRAYER:

It is very easy to remember the bad things that people sometimes do, so help me always to remember their good actions as well.

Stop the Clock!

Kevin was the best runner in the whole school. His friend, Leo, was nearly as good, but sometimes his right ankle let him down, so there was really no one else who could beat Kevin.

Pat often had dreams about beating them both. The dreams were very clear and seemed so real that he was always surprised to wake up and find himself still in bed, but he knew it would never happen for real because he got breathless just running for a bus.

Some of the boys at school made up names for him because he was so fat and would laugh when he had to bend down and pick something up. But Kevin and Leo never laughed at him, and they seemed really pleased when he told them that his dad had given him a stopwatch for his birthday. They said, "Great. You can be the timekeeper for us from now on."

Actually, Pat really didn't want to watch them running because it always made him feel worse, but he was very pleased about the stopwatch because he'd always liked to know how long it took him to get anywhere. In future if he were planning to meet someone, he could get there at just the right time, which was why he was so excited to be going on a school trip to London.

Leo and Kevin were going too, and they arranged to meet at Leo's house first, and to walk together to where the coach would be picking them up. To make sure they would be on the coach by eight o'clock, Pat worked out how long it would take him to have breakfast and to get to Leo's house. He just hoped that his friends wouldn't walk too quickly but decided that if he allowed an extra couple of minutes at his own pace, it would work out all right.

The night before the trip Pat was so excited he hardly slept. He set off even earlier than planned and reached Leo's house at twenty past seven. Nobody came to the door when he knocked, but after a moment, Leo's mum called from a bedroom window and said they'd all overslept and that Leo would catch him up. There was no sign of Kevin at all, so Pat decided to wait another ten minutes, which was the time he had first told Kevin he'd be there, but when Kevin finally turned up, it was almost ten to eight.

"Sorry!" Kevin gasped. "I forgot Leo had moved. I went to his old house. Come on, we'll be all right if we run."

Pat was so angry with his two friends he could hardly speak. Glancing at his watch, he knew there was no way they could reach the coach before twenty past eight. He tried to keep up with Kevin, who was now far ahead, but he was already out of breath and his throat seemed to hurt more with every step. Then, when they were still four streets away from the meeting place, he heard a car pulling up beside them and saw Leo and his father leaning from the window.

"Come on, you two," his dad said. "Hop in. We'll just about make it. I thought you were a good organiser, Pat. Why didn't you allow a bit more time?"

They reached the coach just as it was about to move off, though it wasn't until they were nearly in London that Pat stopped feeling angry. It was so unfair to be told that you hadn't organised things properly when it was other people who had let you down!

In the end, it was a marvellous day in London and after all, he thought, with his new stopwatch he could find out exactly how long it would take them to get home.

PRAYER:

Help me to realise that my actions can affect other people and that it is important to try to keep any promise I make.

Learning the Ropes

Angus was a worrier. He was really quite a beautiful spider if you looked at him in a good light. Soft brown in colour with long, slender legs. However, he had no confidence in himself and felt that he knew nothing about being a successful spider.

Would he ever be able to find enough food? Did he want to live in the corner above the door, or would it be better to choose a spot behind Mrs Wriggler's washing machine?

Angus was always being told that Mrs Wriggler's kitchen was very peaceful and safe. Mrs Wriggler, you see, didn't like doing housework. She hated sweeping and dusting and polishing, so any spider could live there safely without the risk of being disturbed.

Angus was growing bigger and bigger, and getting hungrier and hungrier, but it was no use sitting there worrying. It was time for him to spin his first web! After all, if he wanted to catch some of Mrs Wriggler's kitchen flies, he had to have a proper web of his own. He couldn't carry on as he was . . . forever scuttling about in the dust looking for something to eat. But the big question was, how did one do it? He had tried to see what other spiders did, but they worked so quickly that one minute they were starting on the task and the next, there was a beautiful and elegant piece of lace, so delicate that it swayed each time Mrs Wriggler opened the kitchen door. And where was he going to put a web? It looked very dark and gloomy behind the washing machine and much more interesting in the corner above the kitchen window. He'd be able to see everything from up there. Yes, that was the place to be.

Very carefully, Angus made his way across the floor, making a big detour around Flash, Mrs Wriggler's dog, and the cat basket where Ben, the black cat, always slept. At last he was scaling the curtains, climbing up as far as the pole and clambering over its brass rings, right into the corner where the wall met the ceiling. But he had no idea what to do next.

Then, to his surprise, he saw that on the other side of the window in the far corner, one of his brother spiders was sitting in the centre of a splendid large web.

"Hi there!" said the spider to Angus. "I thought that spot wouldn't stay vacant for very long. Well, don't let me interrupt you. We'll have a word later when you've finished your web."

"Well, actually," said Angus, "I would like a bit of advice," and he told the other spider, very quietly, of course, in case any other spider was listening, about his problem.

"But you know already," said the other spider when he had finished laughing. "It's a talent every spider is born with. Just let it happen. Don't try and think about it so much. Just do it."

Believe it or not, that is exactly what Angus did. He just sat there on the pole and thought hard about the most beautiful web in the world, and before he could stop himself, there it was, a large web spun entirely by him and for him.

"You can have that fly over there if you want," said the other spider. "I've just eaten".

The fly was now coming closer to Angus. Then suddenly he felt a bundle of feathers sweep away the whole of his web, and he found himself being shaken out of the window.

"There you are, mum," said Mrs Wriggler's daughter, waving her new feather duster. "It won't take me long to get your kitchen sorted out. I'll come every Wednesday from now on."

So Angus had to make his way back through the window, and up the curtains again, along to his special place. This time it was very different, now he knew how to spin a web. There was no longer any need to worry. Everything was going to be fine, just so long as he avoided Wednesdays!

PRAYER:

Let me try to remember that worrying about things before they happen doesn't really help.

All in the Family

Olivia sat on the swing and wondered what to do next. Saturday afternoons were so boring and seemed to go on for so long that she often felt they would never end. She could have gone to the supermarket with mum and dad, but that would have been boring too.

If the garden had been more exciting, she would have had lots of things to do, but the two flowerbeds, with their rows of neat geraniums, were as boring as the straight path that went through the middle of the lawn. There was a swing hanging from the branch of the apple tree, but even swinging gets a bit boring if you're doing it on your own. Perhaps, she thought, I could go and find Felix, but as always, Felix was missing.

"I wish I had a cat that stayed at home," she thought. "Or at least someone or something to talk to." Then she heard the sound of a car, and after a moment, she saw her mum in the kitchen.

"Come and help me unpack the shopping," her mum called.

For once, Olivia was pleased to have something to do, and then mum said she was going to do some baking, and after that, the rest of Saturday went much faster.

Soon it was Monday again when she could find out what her friend, Ellie, had been doing that weekend.

"Josh and Harry took me fishing," Ellie said. "Then our cousins came over and mum made a big stew and we played 'Murder' all over the house and then we put on a concert at night for the grown-ups and, on Sunday, we had a barbecue and the family from next door came around. What did you do, Ollie?"

"All sorts of things," said Olivia. "I can't really remember now."

She looked at Ellie's shining face and thought how lucky she was to have brothers and sisters, as well as all those cousins.

During the following week, mum told Olivia that she had a surprise for her. She had invited Ellie to come and stay on Saturday night, and to Olivia's surprise, Ellie seemed delighted at the idea.

"I don't have any cousins or anything," Olivia said, "and mum doesn't like barbecues, but we could go for a walk or something."

"It will be great," said Ellie, and she said it as if she really meant it.

When Saturday came, Olivia was disappointed when mum said that she'd be busy baking all morning, and she went down to the swing to apologise to Ellie who had been swinging since she first arrived.

"We don't have to stay in," she told Ellie. "We could go to the park."

"Mum never has time to bake," Ellie said. "Could we go and watch her?"

"It's a bit boring," Olivia said, "and aren't you tired of swinging by now?"

"I never get a turn on our swing at home," said Ellie. "It must be fantastic to have one of your own."

She had been even more impressed by Olivia's bedroom. "I have to share mine with Sally and Martha," she said. "They're always taking my things and breaking them. Josh and Harry have a room in the attic, and they're always banging on the floor when they know I'm trying to sleep. They think it's a joke, like they did when they spoilt the concert last weekend. Dad gets really mad with them, but mum says teenagers like showing off and that they'll grow up one day. I'd love to live somewhere like this, on my own, with just a mum and dad. You are so lucky, Ollie."

Ellie looked quite sad when she spoke, but later she really enjoyed herself. Ollie's mum let her bake some chocolate cakes to take home, and her dad took them to a film they both wanted to see. She spent hours on the swing in between playing with Felix on the lawn. When she left on Sunday night, she said it was the best weekend she'd ever had.

Afterwards, Olivia told her mum that she wasn't so sure now whether she'd like to be in a big family like Ellie's. Mum said that the grass was always greener on the other side of the fence. Olivia wasn't sure what she meant, but her mum said she liked Ellie a lot and they ought to have her stay again quite soon.

And for once, Olivia agreed with her.

PRAYER:

Help me to enjoy all the good things in my own life and not to envy the way other people live.

Like It Was Before

Midge could hear her brothers' voices from downstairs. Since their new dad had come to live with them, she'd grown used to sitting upstairs in her bedroom until the voices stopped. She knew that the things that Jamie and Luke were saying were the things that she wanted to say to mum. Things like, "Dad never used to make us do that," and, "Why should we go to bed now? Dad always let us stay up later."

Midge sighed. Why didn't Jamie and Luke realise that their new dad was here to stay?

Midge could hear her mother now. "Don't make things more difficult, Jamie. I know how you feel but it will get better, I promise."

Midge couldn't see how that could possibly be true. Their own dad didn't live with them any more, and they only saw him at weekends, so how did mum reckon that things were going to get better? They still thought of their new dad as Mr Roberts, even though mum kept telling them to call him Uncle Bob if that made it easier. But it didn't at all.

At last the voices stopped, and she saw that the boys had gone into the back yard where they kept their bikes. Midge opened the window and shouted.

"Hang on - I'm coming down."

Dad had bought Luke a second-hand bike just before he went away and Luke wouldn't let anyone else even touch it. As Midge reached him, he said, "You can't come with us. We're going on our bikes."

"I know that, but I thought mum said you couldn't."

"Mum didn't say that . . . He did!" said Luke. "We shan't be long."

Midge watched as they wheeled their bikes out of the back gate and thought again of what life had been like before everything had changed. Sometimes she blamed her mother for spoiling things, and the next moment, she would feel angry with her dad. How could he have gone away without them?

Mum must have seen her standing there in the yard, because she came out, drying her hands, "What on earth are we going to do about your brothers?"

Midge was just going to say that she didn't really like Mr Roberts either, when suddenly the back gate opened and Jamie rushed into the yard.

"Mum! Luke's come off his bike! He's run into the side of a car and . . ."

But before he could say anything else mum had rushed out into the street. Midge followed her and saw Luke's bike lying in the gutter and a group of people gathered around a car and its driver.

Luke struggled to his feet. "I'm all right, mum. But look at my bike!"

Midge suddenly saw that Mr Roberts had joined them and was talking to the driver, and writing something on a notepad. Gradually, people moved away and Mr Roberts asked mum to make Luke a hot drink and said that he'd take care of everything. Then he went over to Luke and said, "You've bent the front wheel a bit, but leave it to me. I used to work in a cycle shop. We'll soon get it as good as new."

He didn't say a word about Luke going out on his bike when he'd been told to go to bed, and mum told Midge, afterwards, that he never told Luke that the brakes must have been faulty when dad first bought it.

"I'm afraid your father didn't check it properly," mum said. "But he was so upset about splitting up that he probably forgot. Bob's made me promise not to say anything to Luke though. It was such a lovely present, and he doesn't want anything to upset Luke even more".

Midge thought about this for a long time. She didn't really know her new dad yet, but it sounded as if he was already on Luke's side and that seemed to be a good sign. She thought for a while. Maybe it might not be too difficult for them to call him 'Uncle Bob' once they'd all grown used to him being around.

PRAYER: ══

Unexpected changes in our lives are often unwelcome so
help me to understand that learning to accept them will make
them seem less frightening.

Flying Freddy

A butterfly was resting on the blue spray of flowers above Freddy's head. He had been watching it for a long time from his favourite place at the edge of the pond. The butterfly must have known he was being watched and tried to show how clever it was.

First it swooped down to a flower quite near to Freddy's head, and then it flew across to a hollyhock on the other side of the garden, then hovered over some red roses and a peony before flying up to the blue flowers at the top of the bush.

"If only I could fly like that," thought Freddy. "I'd become the most famous frog in the whole world, but I never shall. I'm only a very ordinary frog."

As he sat there thinking, he heard a loud croak. He always knew his best friend's croak as soon as he heard it.

"Monty!" he said. "How long have you been under that water-lily?"

"For ages and ages," said Monty. "It's so cool and shady, and I wanted to rest because I've been practising my forward leap all morning and it's very exhausting."

On hearing this, Freddy felt even more depressed. Monty had become the best jumper from all the year's tadpoles, and no other frog could ever hope to compete with him. Freddy could jump, of course, but knowing he would never be as good as Monty somehow took away all his enthusiasm, so for most of the time, he just sat by the edge of the pond and watched butterflies.

"Done any good jumps lately?" said Monty.

Freddy looked at him sadly. "I'm not really interested in jumping," he said. "What I'd really like to do is to fly like that butterfly up there."

"You were always complaining even when you were a tadpole," Monty said. "And now you're even worse. Why can't you just enjoy being a frog?"

Without any warning, Monty disappeared again under the water-lily, just as two boys reached the edge of the pond. Freddy knew about boys and their habits. He knew they threw stones and often went to the river with fishing nets and carried jam jars tied up with string.

This time, though, they stopped by the pond and looked closely into the water. "Look over there! Something moved under that water-lily. I think it's a frog!"

Then the other boy said, "And there's another one there, just near your foot."

Freddy's heart leapt into his mouth as he saw a fishing net suddenly come rushing down towards him. With a gigantic effort, he shot upwards, diving past the boy's legs, aiming for the safety of a clump of nettles beyond the water's edge. To his surprise, he found himself soaring over the nettles towards the bush with the trailing blue flowers. He just couldn't believe it! He was flying! Because he had been so afraid, he had made the biggest jump of his whole life.

"So this is what real jumping is all about," he thought. "If I'd known it was so exciting I'd have done it before."

He landed under the lower branches of the bush, but he was near enough to hear the boys laughing and to be amazed and delighted by what one of them said.

"Did you see that? I've never seen a frog leap so high!"

Afterwards, Monty couldn't believe the boys had said such a thing, but Freddy knew that he was impressed, because he invited Freddy to join him under the water-lily, something Monty had never done before.

But Freddy had other plans. "I'm sorry," he said. "I'm afraid I'm far too busy. I have to practise my forward leap, and you know how exhausting that is!"

PRAYER:

*Help me to remember that I can often achieve much more than
I believe I can and that I need not be afraid of challenges.*

Tatters

Ellie thought Tatters was the best dog in the whole world. Her uncle had bought him as a puppy but decided that as he was away so much it would be better if he came to live with Ellie. Now she couldn't even remember what it was like to be without him. She and mum had bought him a basket, a nice new lead and collar, and once he'd stopped missing his brother puppies, he settled down happily and wanted to be with Ellie wherever she went.

Mum had been to the library and brought home a book about bringing up puppies, and she explained to Ellie how he'd have to be taken to the vet's to have further injections.

"We'll be able to take him there together," said mum. "I've made the appointment for half term."

Ellie had never been to a vet's before and was fascinated to see all the different animals with their owners. In the waiting room, there was a cat in a basket, a tortoise in a box, a guinea pig in a little cage, and even a goldfish in a large round bowl.

Before they had even sat down, she could see that Tatters wanted to go home. He was pulling very hard on his lead and looked nothing like the happy dog who had just been playing in the garden.

"Does he really have to have injections, mum?" Ellie said. "You can see he doesn't like coming here."

"He'll be all right with Mr Downing," said mum, and told Ellie not to fuss. But when their turn came, Ellie could hardly pull Tatters into the surgery. He sat on his haunches and refused to move, so mum and Mr Downing had to lift him up on to the table. Ellie had never seen him look so unhappy, and she hated it when the vet held him still and gave him the injection, while Tatters whimpered and struggled to get free. Once they were home, he soon recovered, but it was Ellie who begged mum never to take him to the vet's again.

"We must keep him fit and healthy," said mum. "Next time you can stay at home if you like."

Before the next appointment at the vet's, something happened to Tatters. At first they noticed that he sometimes rubbed the side of his face along the floor, and they laughed because he'd never done that before. Then he began to do it more often, and sometimes he whimpered and turned away from his food.

Mum looked at the dog book again, and they watched him very carefully for the next few days. He no longer seemed to want to play with his ball and didn't lift his head when they suggested a walk. At last, mum said she would have to take him to the vet's again.

"I know you don't want to come this time," mum said. "But don't worry. We'll be back soon."

Tatters came across to Ellie and pushed against her knee as he always did when he wanted to play, but his eyes looked very sad, and when she stroked his face, he pulled away from her quickly.

"I think he wants me to come too," said Ellie, and she reluctantly went to get her coat. As they walked into the vet's, she had the same sinking feeling in her stomach as Tatters began to pull at his lead just as before. But after lifting him on to the table, Mr Downing shone a light down Tatters' throat and said, "Mystery solved! All right, old boy. We'll soon have you comfortable again."

Then he said to Ellie, "Come and have a look. No wonder he's been so unhappy."

Ellie bent over and peered into Tatters' mouth. A narrow splinter of bone had trapped itself between two teeth, inflaming the gums and piercing the roof of his mouth. Mum looked too and said, "It must have been one of the chicken bones he found last week near the litter bin in the park. He'd grabbed them before Ellie could stop him, but we didn't realise he'd chewed any."

In a moment, the vet had removed the bone and Tatters was on the floor, leaping up at Ellie and barking with excitement. He even leapt up at Mr Downing and tried to pull at his white coat as if he wanted to play.

Perhaps now, thought Ellie, he won't mind coming here next time. Certainly she wouldn't, because now she could see that, thanks to the vet, Tatters was his old self again . . . the best dog in the whole world.

PRAYER:

It's not always easy to know how we can help our pets when they are ill or distressed, but help me to remember how much they rely on us for their well-being.

Katy's Kitten

Katy longed to have a pet. She didn't mind what kind of animal it was. All she wanted was something of her own. Something she could feed and look at and touch, but dad said there was no way they could keep an animal in their tiny flat. The flat was near the hospital where Katy's mum was staying, and dad said that living there was better than having to make the long journey every day from where they'd lived before.

At first Katy liked the flat because they had to go in a lift to the sixth floor before they could open their front door. She also liked her bedroom, because out of its window she could see the roof of the hospital where mum was. At least she didn't have to go to another school because dad took her every morning in his van, and every teatime he collected her from her friend Midge's house. This was a part of the day that Katy loved because Midge had a dog, and an old cat called Stripy, as well as two white mice and a rabbit.

Katy had pleaded with her father for a long time. "There'd be room for a tiny cage, just for one mouse," she said.

"And I'd be the one who'd have to clean it out and feed it after the first week," he said. "No, Katy. I've enough on my plate at the moment. Please don't go on about it."

Then one Saturday morning, when she went to get dad's paper, she walked back a different way and passed a row of houses she'd never seen before. On the front of the end one was the sign 'Animal Shelter', and when she peered into its garden she could see a line of kennels. She heard a car stop and a lady carrying a large box climbed out and came up to the front gate.

"Another four kittens," she said. "Oh well, I suppose we'll find room for them somewhere. We generally do." She smiled at Katy. "Do you know anyone who might like one?"

She held out the box, and Katy saw four black kittens half hidden in a large blanket.

Katy reached down and touched one of the small heads. "Dad says we haven't any room for a pet." The kitten felt warm, and she wanted to lift it out of the box so she could feel its weight on her hands, but the lady said, "I'm sorry. I'll have to get them inside now, but if your father ever changes his mind, come and see us."

"Have you always got animals here?"

"We have indeed. Some of the dogs have been with us for years, but we always try and find good homes if we can."

Katy touched the kitten for the last time. Already it felt like her own special kitten, but there was no way dad was going to change his mind. She walked very slowly back to the flat. Never had she wanted anything so much, and never before had she felt so angry and hurt. It might have been easier if she'd never seen the kitten, she thought. That night, she cried into her pillow and felt too angry to talk to her father. The next evening, though, when they visited mum, they found her in a different part of the hospital.

"They put me in here because they're short of space," she said. "I'll be coming home soon, but these ladies have all been here for a long time and might never be able to go home."

Katy was still feeling unhappy about the kitten, but then, as she perched on the bed, she suddenly saw the lady from the Animal Shelter. She was leading a large sheepdog towards one of the beds, and Katy watched as he was led from bed to bed to greet each old lady in turn. They all seemed very pleased to see him. Then at last the lady reached mum's bed. She recognised Katy at once.

"Hello again!" she said. "This is Bruno. He's very old now but he enjoys his visits to see his friends. Actually we've still got two more wards to do. Would you like to come round with us?"

Katy looked at dad and he said, "Off you go. I've got lots of things to tell mum." So Katy took Bruno's lead, and felt really proud because everybody made such a fuss of him as they walked through the wards. It felt as if he were her own dog.

"I think Bruno's magic," she told dad later. "He made everyone feel better." And she knew it was true because somehow she felt better too.

PRAYER:

Disappointments can hurt a lot but help me to put them behind me and to look forward to the good things ahead.

Joining Hands

Dad kept everything in the garage. There were step ladders, garden tools, boxes of screws, paint pots and brushes, old hammers, tea-chests, spray cans, flower pots - everything you could think of, together with empty boxes for the toaster, the computer, the lawn mower and mum's coffee pot, which dad said might be needed one day if they ever moved.

Sometimes there was no space at all left for the car, so it had to stand outside in the drive until dad had taken all the extra rubbish to the tip. This didn't happen very often, so for most of the time, dad let Josh and his friends, Callum and Kirsty, play in the garage whenever it was raining. Kirsty, who lived next door, used to bring around an old suitcase full of dressing up clothes, and Josh would choose whether they would become spacemen, pirates or gangsters for the afternoon. Generally, he and Kirsty would pick out all the best clothes, so that Callum was told he'd got to be a refugee or a beggar and put on the ones that were left. He always grumbled about this, until one day he decided that he was really a very important character who was only wearing the rags because he was in disguise, and that made him feel better.

One Saturday afternoon, while they were playing, mum came into the garage and said she was looking for an old saucepan that had gone missing. She began to tug at all the boxes which toppled down in a great heap against the step ladder on which dad had balanced a box of half empty paint tins. Kirsty leapt out of the way as the tins crashed down, upsetting a stack of plant pots which scattered over a pile of newspapers that mum had saved for recycling.

"Perhaps my old saucepan is behind the lawn mower," mum said, as if she hadn't noticed all the mess around her. "Callum, can you give me a hand?"

She and Callum tugged at the mower, but its cord was caught up in a tangle of old electrical fittings that dad was keeping in case they came in useful one day.

"Bother!" said mum. "We'll have to get it right out."

As they freed the mower from all the flexes and cords, she suddenly gave a cry of delight. "There's my old clothes-line!" she said. "I wondered where it had gone. Kirsty, could you reach it? It's behind that bag of compost."

The bag of compost must have been opened before, because as Kirsty pulled out the clothes-line, the bag toppled forward, and compost poured out over her feet.

It was at that moment that dad came into the garage. First he looked at mum, and then at Josh and Callum, and finally at Kirsty, who was standing in the centre of what had once been an empty floor.

"We came to play at gangsters," Josh said quickly, "because it's raining."

"And I came to look for my old saucepan," said mum.

"The compost bag must have been open at the top," said Kirsty.

They'd expected him to be cross because of all the mess, but they saw that he was smiling.

"It looks like an earthquake," he said. "But this should teach me to keep the garage tidier in future."

"How on earth are we going to tidy it all up?" said mum. "Where do we start?"

"We start," said dad, "with a cup of tea, and then we'll join forces. We'll put everything out into the drive first, and then we'll decide what we really need to keep and how to arrange it along each wall."

"But it will take ages," said Josh. "We shan't have time to play our gangsters game."

Dad grinned. "Cheer up. You know what they say. Many hands make light work. With ten hands between us, we'll have it done in a jiffy."

It did take a little longer than a jiffy, but when the tidying was all done, they could hardly recognise the garage. Dad went to the tip, and Josh, Callum and Kirsty finished their game long before he came back to put the car inside again. And best of all, mum found her old saucepan behind one of the tea-chests. So it turned out to be, as Josh said afterwards, quite a good Saturday afternoon after all.

PRAYER:

Help me to remember that working together with other people can overcome difficulties that would be hard to face alone.

Dragon in the Hedge

Emily looked at mum and sighed, "Do we have to take George with us?"

"Well, of course we do," said mum. "You can't leave babies on their own. Cheer up. I thought you liked picking blackberries."

"I do," said Emily. "But George always cries and spoils things."

This time, though, George behaved himself and slept in his pram all through the long afternoon. It was very hot between the high hedges of their favourite lane where all the best blackberries grew, and when Emily's small basket was nearly full of berries, she decided to walk towards a clump of trees where it looked cool and shady.

"That's a good idea," dad said. "Take George with you. We'll catch you up."

It was difficult to push such a big pram along the bumpy lane, and Emily began to feel even hotter. After a short time, she stopped to look back. There was no sign of mum and dad, although she thought she could hear their voices. George was still asleep, and she almost wished she could wake him up to show him how far she had pushed him. But he went on sleeping. The lane seemed very quiet.

"We'll go back now," she said aloud, and began to turn the pram, but however hard she tried, she couldn't move it. Then she saw that one of its wheels was caught in a bramble. She bent down to free it, when suddenly she heard a sound. It was an odd, rustling, pushing kind of noise. Something very large was trying to force its way into the lane from the other side of the hedge. One of the bushes began to move and the rustling sound grew louder. She could see something now through the branches. It was brown and very big.

"Mum!" she shouted, "Dad!"

George woke up at once and began to cry. Then he saw her basket full of big ripe blackberries, and he stopped crying and made a grab for it. Instantly, the basket fell over the edge of the pram into the long grass. Emily gave the pram a last, angry push, and it tilted suddenly on to its two front wheels. George gave a cry of alarm, and Emily quickly lifted him free.

"Don't cry," she said. "It's all right."

But she knew it wasn't all right. The crunching noise in the hedge was much closer now and very loud! Gasping, she began to run back along the lane, trying all the time not to drop George.

"Mum!" she called again.

Suddenly she saw her mother step out from behind some bushes.

Emily flung George into her arms. "The pram tipped up and there was something in the hedge and George spilt all my blackberries and I thought you'd gone home without me."

Her father put down his basket. "What do you mean 'something in the hedge'?"

"It was big and brown and I could hear it snorting. It sounded like a dragon."

"Then we'd better go and have a look," said dad.

Together they all walked back along the lane. Mum carried George, and Emily held her father's hand very tightly. Everything was very quiet.

When they reached the pram, dad freed it from the bramble and mum plumped up George's pillow and settled him down again. Then dad quickly lifted Emily and set her firmly on to his left shoulder.

"You'll get a good view of the dragon from up there," he said.

She was now so high that she could see over the hedge into the wide field beyond. The field was empty apart from four brown cows that were slowly walking away from the hedge.

"Any sign of him?" said dad.

"Er - no. No, there isn't," said Emily.

"It's not every day you meet a dragon," said dad, putting her down on to the ground again. "You were very brave to rescue George."

Emily knew she would have to tell him about the cows later but she felt she wasn't quite ready.

"I wasn't really brave," she said, "because I think it was only a small one."

PRAYER:

Everybody knows what it's like to be afraid, but help me to understand that sometimes we imagine things to be worse than they really are.

My Friend Ben

My friend Ben always wins races. I don't like losing, but I know that if Ben is in the same race, he'll be the one who wins every time. When he runs he makes it look so easy, and he never gets out of breath like I do. I'd love to be like Ben.

Anyway, something happened yesterday that had never happened before. In the middle of the race, Ben fell down. I thought I was near the back, but I passed him before he could get to his feet. Suddenly I realised that there were only two boys in front of me. I've never run so fast in my life. My throat hurt and I had a pain in my side, but I could see the teachers holding the tape and the next thing, there I was - the winner!

It was fantastic and I looked round to check whether Ben had seen it, but he was still half way down the track, sitting on the ground.

"I won!" I said. "Did you see?"

Ben grunted something and bent over his shoe again. "It was these trainers," he said. "The laces came undone. My last ones didn't have laces, just that sticky stuff."

I knew how fed up he'd been when his mother had told him he couldn't have any new ones and would have to use a pair that had belonged to his brother. She said they'd hardly been worn and that she couldn't afford to get Ben another pair at the moment. I knew he hated wearing them, and now that he'd lost a race for the first time ever, he was going to hate them even more.

Ben looked up suddenly and said, "Can you tie them? I can't."

Then I remembered - once or twice before he'd asked me to help, but he'd always made an excuse about his hands being too cold or something.

"Don't tell anyone," he said.

So I tied them for him and said I wouldn't tell. I couldn't believe that someone like Ben still found it hard to tie a shoelace.

As we went back into the playground, there was loud barking. A big black dog had come through a gap in the fence and was rushing towards us. I hate big dogs, and I started to run.

"It's only Blackie," said Ben. "He lives near us," and he laughed as Blackie leapt up at him, nearly knocking him over. He must have seen my face and said, "You're not scared of dogs, are you?"

I couldn't tell him that I was, especially big ones, because at that moment a lady came running into the playground, holding a lead.

"Oh Ben, thank you for grabbing him. He slipped out of his collar before I could stop him. Come here, Blackie, you wicked dog!"

Already a crowd of boys had gathered around so nobody noticed that I'd moved away. Minutes later, she led Blackie away on his lead and Ben came over to me. He didn't seem to mind about me being afraid of big dogs, although he did say he couldn't understand why I was. But then, I suppose I don't understand about him being afraid to tell anyone that he's not very good at tying shoelaces. So, in a way, we're quits.

It's really great having him as my best friend. In fact, the next time we're in a race together, I'm going to check his shoelaces before we start, just to make sure that he's the winner.

PRAYER:

Help me to understand that everybody has difficulties to face and that we each find our own way of learning to cope with them.

All in the Dark

For the very first time, Jessica was going to be away from home on her birthday, and mum had told her that this year there would be no party because she'd be staying at Gran's.

She had explained it all to Jessica who could see that it wasn't mum's fault. After all, mum hadn't asked the hospital to fix that date for her to have an operation, and Jessica could hardly stop at home on her own.

"You'll enjoy being at Gran's," said mum. "You'll be able to play with Whiskers again and look at all Gran's treasures."

Jessica agreed that she would, although mum always made things sound better than they really were. Whiskers was gran's old cat, and all he seemed to do was sleep. Gran's so-called treasures were just a few things in a shoebox that she'd collected over the years.

What mum didn't know though, was that Jessica had never liked gran's house. It was very dark and had stone steps down to a cellar, as well as two dusty attics full of cobwebs and old suitcases. Sometimes Jessica used to ask Gran if she could go to bed early, which meant that she could be safely tucked up in bed while it was still light and didn't have to walk along the landing which was even darker than the stairs.

She had never told mum anything about this, so she was surprised when mum said, "Take my little torch. Then you'll be able to see those two steps up to Gran's bathroom. I always forget they're there and trip over."

Jessica had never seen her mum trip over anything, but she took the torch and it made her feel better straight away. She still wasn't looking forward to her birthday and felt awful inside when she kissed mum goodbye the day before.

Gran's house hadn't changed at all. It still smelt musty and not at all like home, but it was good to see Whiskers again, and Jessica was pleased when he came to sit on her knee before she went to bed. She tried to put off going upstairs for as long as she could, but at last Gran said, "Off you go now. Up the wooden hill."

Jessica said, "You always say that," but as she spoke, the light suddenly went out.

"Oh no!" said Gran. "Not another power cut! I meant to get some more candles, but I forgot. I'll just check the television in case it's only the bulb in the lamp."

But the television was dead, and when they groped their way into the kitchen, there was no sound of the electric clock on the wall. Even the refrigerator had gone quiet.

"You'd better get your case upstairs," said Gran. "I think I'll have an early night too. What a pity. I haven't even shown you my treasures yet."

Jessica shivered. How could she tell Gran that she didn't want to go up to that dark landing on her own or face the blackness of the bedroom? Then she remembered.

"I've got mum's torch in my case," she said. Unzipping it, she reached down into the bag, feeling her way past her dressing gown and slippers, until she reached the torch. With a quick switch, Jessica waved the beam of light into the darkness.

"That's better," said Gran. Then she gave Jessica a very odd smile and said, "I think it's a bit early for bed, don't you? Why don't we start your birthday tonight instead of tomorrow? If you'll guide me across to the dresser I think we can add even more light."

Jessica didn't know what she was talking about, but on the dresser she could see something covered with a cloth. Carefully, Gran selected two plates and took out a box of matches from the drawer. Finally she lifted the cloth.

"A birthday cake!" said Jessica.

"I made it yesterday. Now, if you'll keep shining the torch I'll light the candles." As the seven candles were lit, the whole kitchen began to glow with light, and Jessica felt she was sitting in a strange and magical cave. Even Whiskers came in to see what was happening.

Jessica watched her Gran starting to cut the cake. There was no doubt about it. It was going to be a really great birthday!

PRAYER:

Help me to remember that even at the darkest times, one small light is enough to make the blackness disappear.

Keeping Quiet

Mia liked to watch people talking. If they spoke English quickly, it still sounded far too difficult, but since she'd started at her new school, she was slowly beginning to understand the things they were saying. Each evening she would write down the new words for her parents to learn, because she already knew far more than they did. After all, she had teachers and new friends to meet every day, but they didn't.

She liked her teacher, Miss Robinson, who had red hair and wore the colours that Mia liked too - reds and blues and sometimes a long skirt of green that looked like English grass.

"Learning someone else's language is always difficult, Mia, but you're doing really well," she'd say. Then she'd laugh. "Having Kylie as a friend must have helped a lot."

Mia nodded, pleased with herself for understanding most of the words. But even when she understood, she always felt afraid of speaking a reply out loud. Everybody knew Kylie, because she never stopped talking and she seemed to have more friends than anyone else in the school.

Kylie had stayed with Mia ever since that first day when Miss Robinson had sat them both together. Kylie was her special friend, so Mia wanted to say, "Yes, I like Kylie. She makes me laugh so much. She tells me everything about the things she does, and about all her brothers and sisters, and one day, I want to tell her everything about my home and coming to live in England, and about the things I'm thinking, just as she tells me."

However, although she wanted to say those things, she found that all the words she thought she had learned just melted away, or she put them in the wrong order, or her tongue seemed to make them sound different from how Kylie said them, so all she could do was smile and nod.

At school, Kylie never seemed to be on her own, so Mia was surprised one day when she found her in the cloakroom, staring out of the window. Mia cleared her throat.

"Kylie?"

Kylie was startled. "I didn't know you were there," she said.

Mia could see that she had been crying, but as always she hesitated, searching for the words she needed.

Kylie blew her nose and said, "I'm all right. It's just dad. He's left us and he's not going to come back."

Mia nodded. "Your dad . . ." Then she stopped. The words had escaped again, leaving her standing there, silent and feeling stupid. She reached out a hand and touched Kylie's arm.

"Thanks, Mia," Kylie said, "I knew you'd understand. I told someone else on the way to school, and they never stopped telling me about how their father had left them years ago, and how pleased they were that he'd gone. They made me feel worse than ever, and I bet they go round telling everybody else now. I just wish I'd never told them. But you're different. That's why I like telling you things. You just listen all the time, and you listen so hard that I know everything I'm saying is just as important to you as it is to me."

She spoke so quickly that Mia found it difficult to understand every word, but she could tell that there was no question for her to answer at the end.

She knew the moment was a special one, and she wanted to say something. Then she remembered what Miss Robinson had often said about learning a new language. At least some of those words hadn't escaped her.

"It is always diffi - difficult," she said carefully.

Kylie stared at her in surprise.

"I am sorry," said Mia. "Your dad . . ." And then all the new English words she was learning seemed to disappear again. But she could see that Kylie was smiling now.

"I'll have to keep my eye on you, Mia," Kylie said. "We'll soon be having to shut you up!"

Mia laughed too. She didn't quite know why Kylie wanted to lock her up, but it didn't really matter. One day soon, she'd be able to understand an English joke whenever Kylie told her one.

PRAYER:

Help me to understand how difficult it is to learn someone else's language and to welcome newcomers who are far away from their own homes.

Robert's Zoo

Erica always wished that she'd had a brother her own age. She wouldn't have minded one even younger. At least they could have played together. But Robert was sixteen and he was almost as tall as dad. Sometimes she almost forgot that she had a brother, because he seemed so grown up, but that was before last summer when Robert went out on his bike and never came back. Now she can never forget him.

That was when Erica found out how much it hurt to think about him. She couldn't make it stop hurting because what had happened to Robert was real, and there was nothing anyone could do about it.

The day it happened had been just like any other day in the school holidays. Erica's friend, Clare, had come around to play and Robert had gone out on his bike with his friends. He'd come into the garden to tell mum that he wouldn't be home until the afternoon because they were going to cycle up to Eagle Crag and picnic up there. Mum was hanging out some washing and said, "Take care," as she always did, and Robert had given Erica's swing a big push so that she nearly fell off.

Erica always hated being pushed like that, so she'd called after Robert as he ran off and said that she hoped it would rain and that he'd get a puncture. Clare had laughed and told Erica that she was lucky to have a big brother like Robert because he was always so nice and friendly.

That was all over now because on that summer afternoon, the police had come to tell mum that a lorry on the hill near Eagle Crag had killed Robert. Even after the funeral Erica couldn't really believe that she would never see him again. It must have been some sort of mistake! She knew what it felt like when people died, because gran had gone into hospital and never came home again. But gran had been very old, and she had said how tired and lonely she was without grandpa, so you really couldn't be too unhappy.

But someone like Robert? Whenever Erica felt sad, mum would tell her to remember all the good times she'd had with him. She said that was why you never really lose the people you love. But however hard Erica tried, nothing seemed to take the pain away. Then one day, mum said they were going to take a picnic up to Eagle Crag. They'd always had family picnics up there for as long as Erica could remember, but they hadn't been there since last summer. Dad seemed to think it wasn't a good idea, but off they went. It was a very windy day just like the one when Robert had gone on that last cycle ride.

They parked the car at the top of the hill and had a long walk, right over Eagle Crag towards the reservoir. In the shelter of a stone wall they sat down to have their picnic.

"Just look at all those clouds," said mum. "They're moving so quickly and they're changing shape all the time."

It was then that Erica remembered another picnic she and Robert had gone on their own, but on their way back they had missed the bus and had to wait for a long time. Erica had felt cold and tired until Robert had told her to watch the clouds racing across the sky.

"We're in a zoo, look! That one's an elephant," he'd said, "and now it's changing into a camel".

Erica had loved joining in. "That one's a tiger - and that one there is a giraffe."

Remembering how he'd made her laugh, she found herself smiling and when mum asked her why, she said, "It's Robert's Zoo again. Look - there's a tiger."

Mum laughed too, "I'd forgotten. He used to play that game when he was very small. Thank you for reminding me."

For the first time, Erica realised that mum had been right about remembering people, because she knew now, that on any windy day in future, when she saw clouds, she would think about Robert again without it hurting so much.

PRAYER:

Help me to realise that even when someone has died, we can make sure that they remain part of our lives by remembering the happiness they gave us.

Meeting Mollie

Rose was six. In fact it was nearly time for another birthday and she was longing for it to come quickly so that she could say that she was seven. She had the day marked on the calendar in her bedroom and had drawn a big ring around June 16th with a red crayon.

It was already June, so she hadn't many more days to go. But this year mum had asked her if she'd mind if she had her party a few weeks after the 16th, because the new baby would be arriving about the same time and she might be too busy to make cakes and jellies or anything.

Rose thought that her mum was making far too much fuss about something that hadn't happened yet, and didn't take too much notice when dad fetched her old cot down from the attic. Each day she ticked off the calendar until, at last, bedtime on the 15th of June finally arrived. Mum had gone upstairs with her, and she called to Rose from the top of the stairs.

"Everything's ready now. Come and see."

Rose went eagerly into mum's bedroom thinking that perhaps she was going to get her presents now, but all she could see was mum's weekend case on the bed.

"Look - aren't these lovely?" mum said. She lifted up a small white jacket, and some miniature bootees.

Disappointed, Rose said, "Are we still going to have a baby then?"

Mum patted her tummy and said, "Yes, of course, we are. Aren't you excited?"

Rose knew where babies came from, but she was surprised that mum seemed so sure about it. "Not really," she said. "I'd like to stay as we are."

Mum closed the case. "Aunty Pat's coming tonight, and she'll stay until I come home. It should only be a few days," and she gave Rose a big hug then said, "Your party will be a really special one this year, won't it?"

Later, Rose heard a taxi stop outside, and when she ran to the window, she saw dad helping mum into the back seat. She didn't want to see it drive away and was pleased when Aunty Pat came up to say goodnight.

At half past six in the morning, they were both wakened by the telephone, and after a few minutes, Aunty Pat came rushing into the bedroom.

"You've got a little sister!" she said. "She was born at five o'clock this morning, and we can go and see her this afternoon."

The postman came with lots of cards, and Rose opened all her presents, plus the one from Aunty Pat, as well as the chocolates from her friend Martha. But somehow it didn't seem like a birthday.

When they got to the hospital, mum looked very excited. She was wearing a new bed jacket, and there was a cot beside her.

"Come and meet Mollie," she said.

Rose looked down into the cot. Mollie's tiny hands looked like two small starfish.

"Can I touch her?" said Rose. Mollie's fingers curled round Rose's thumb, gripping it firmly.

"Aren't I lucky?" said Aunty Pat. "I've got two nieces, but I shall only have one date to mark on the calendar."

Rose felt lucky too when she suddenly realised that not only had they got a new baby, but she was also now a big sister who was seven years old!

PRAYER:

*Help me to learn to try to welcome a newcomer into the family
even when I don't want things to change.*

Getting Better

Sam's mother always seemed to be taking him to the doctor's. At least that was what Jacob and Charlie thought.

"He goes there nearly every week," said Jacob.

"And every week he tells us about it. If he hasn't a bad cold then he's got spots."

Jacob laughed. "And when he has spots they're so tiny you can hardly see them."

Charlie felt pleased that he and Jacob never had to go to the doctor's. They were both tall and strong, and they never seemed to catch colds or have spots. Charlie was a very good swimmer, and Jacob was the best skate-boarder in the whole class, so they never wanted to spend much time with Sam, who was always telling them how his leg hurt or how sore his throat was.

So they were surprised when Sam asked them to go with him to see a film on his birthday.

"Mum's taking us to have a burger first," he said. "Then she's booked us seats for the matinee. I hope I'm all right, because I think I might be getting a cold."

"Surprise, surprise!" said Jacob.

Charlie giggled but all Sam said was, "Come over to our house first and don't be late."

Afterwards, Charlie and Jacob felt quite guilty that they'd teased Sam about his cold, because all that week he had a really bad one. But by Saturday he was better, and his mother took them to the big new cafe in the High Street and let them have anything they wanted. Jacob and Charlie had double burgers, as well as fries and two glasses of pop, followed by chocolate muffins and ice-cream. She even bought them popcorn later, and said they could stop for some chips at the local fish and chip shop on their way home.

Charlie began to wish his own mum was more like her. Then during the night, he woke up feeling awful. His stomach hurt, and, after he'd been to the bathroom twice to be sick, his throat hurt too and he felt hot and shivery. Mum stayed up all night with him because he made such a fuss.

"I think it could be food poisoning," she said. "I'll ring Sam's mother in the morning and see whether he's the same, and then if you're no better I'll ring the doctor."

Charlie thought she was beginning to sound like Sam's mother, but for the first time ever he decided he ought to see the doctor. All he needed, he thought, was for something to stop him being sick and having these awful pains.

In the morning though, mum checked with both Sam and Jacob's mothers, and was told that Sam and Jacob were perfectly all right.

"Are you going to ring the doctor then?" said Charlie.

"Well, it is Sunday," said his mum, "and you don't seem too bad. Let's see how you are tomorrow. Make sure you drink lots of water and I'm sure you'll soon feel better."

It was the longest and dreariest day that Charlie had ever known. Jacob came around to see if he wanted to play in the park. Then Sam came to ask if they both wanted to go to his house to watch his new birthday videos. But Charlie said he wasn't feeling well enough, and began telling them how awful it had been in the night, and how his throat hurt, and how he still had this pain in his stomach. They hardly seemed to be listening. Didn't they realise how ill he was feeling?

All day he lay in bed feeling sorry for himself. How could mum sit downstairs watching television? And why didn't Jacob stay with him instead of rushing off with Sam to see the video?

Thinking about Sam, he began to wonder if this was what Sam often felt like, wanting to have someone listen to him when he was ill. Perhaps in the future, he could try to listen a bit more. After all, it had been good that Sam had invited him to watch that film - he'd wanted to see it for months, and it wasn't Sam's fault that he'd been sick.

Maybe a bit later he'd go downstairs and watch television. Yes, he was definitely feeling better! He might even manage a bowl of cereal once he'd finished reading his new comic.

PRAYER:

Help me to appreciate my good health but also to remember how quickly we forget how it feels to be ill once we are well again.

Caring for the Countryside

Crisps and packs and instant snacks,
Plastic coil and silver foil,
Bottles, sprays and freezer trays-
TAKE THEM HOME!

Fish and chips and paper clips,
Pet-food cans and rubber bands,
Plastic forks and bottle corks -
TAKE THEM HOME!

Rotting bags and dirty rags,
Metal rings and jagged things,
Broken china, dustbin liner -
PLEASE - TAKE THEM HOME!

BUT....

Bluebell, Buttercup and Thyme, curling fern and bramble vine,
Cowslip, Orchid, Daisies white, scented Honeysuckle bright
Ragged Robin, Violets blue, Shepherd's Purse, and Poppies too -
Guard them well and let them stay, safe to grace another day.
DON'T TAKE THEM HOME!

The Knife

Edmund stood on the hill and looked down at the village. This time the Romans had driven away the raiders from the north, and now there was peace again for the people who lived in the houses around the Great Wall.

Edmund's father was very old, but the Romans paid him well for his hunting dogs, and now Edmund had brought the last two puppies for the Commandant of the fort. He had cared for the dogs since they were born and had hated the idea of going home without them, but they were now almost fully grown and the long journey to the Wall had made them restless and disobedient. In a way, it would be a relief to hand them over to someone else. He had travelled for two days to reach the fort and was pleased when the raiders were finally driven off and he could carry out his father's instructions to go to the smith's house, close by the Wall.

The smith seemed surprised to see him. "You'll have to wait for the Commandant to return from a hunting trip," he said, "but you can stay here tonight. I know your father well and am sorry that he can no longer make such a journey."

As he settled down to sleep, Edmund held his knife closely to his chest. It had belonged to his father who had passed it on to him, so it was now his most precious possession. He was still carrying it the following morning when he saw a big party of horsemen returning to the fort and noticed a Roman boy, about his own age, go to greet the riders. He was holding a slender hound on a leash, and when he saw Edmund staring in surprise he said, "Haven't you seen a dog before?"

"Not one as thin as that. Is it a hunting dog?"

The boy laughed. "It ought to be, but she never catches anything. She's far too gentle. I saw you yesterday. You're the boy who's brought the dogs for my father."

"Your father?"

"The Commandant. I'm his eldest son, Flavius. Come on, let's give her a run. The clerk won't have your money ready yet."

Edmund hesitated, but Flavius tugged his arm and said, "Come on . . . you'll see how fast she goes."

The two boys climbed the hill while the dog chased imaginary hares until she flopped down beside them, exhausted. Flavius took an apple from his tunic and said,

"We could share it if we had a knife."

Edmund wondered whether his father would believe that he had this new friend, the son of an important Roman.

"Look, I have one," he said, and handed over the knife.

Flavius cut the apple and said, "I wish I had a knife like that, even though it has such a plain bone handle. Would you give it to me?"

"No," said Edmund. "It was my father's knife. I shall keep it always."

Flavius shrugged and then said, "Look, she thinks she's found another hare."

The boys raced after her, and they spent the whole morning together, until Flavius said, "I shall be going home soon. My father is sending me back."

"Home?"

"To Rome. Come on, I'll race you back."

Following him, Edmund realised that he might never see Flavius again; yet it felt as if he had known him all his life. Then he suddenly remembered. Flavius still had his knife! He began to call, but Flavius was already inside the Fort, lost in the crowds around the gateway. Then he saw the smith hurrying towards him. "The Commandant is very pleased with your dogs," he said. "You will get your money if you go to the clerk's office this afternoon."

"But my knife? Flavius has my knife!"

"You deserve to lose it if you trust a Roman," said the smith.

Sadly, Edmund collected his money and set off on the long journey home, but after half an hour, he heard a shout and turned to see a horseman racing towards him. He handed over a packet wrapped in a cloth, and inside Edmund felt the shape of a knife. It was his own knife, but when he touched the handle, it no longer felt smooth. Carved into the bone, a slender hound now raced towards its tip where a small, fleeting hare escaped from it forever.

Looking back towards the Fort, Edmund thought again of Flavius, the friend he would never forget. Flavius must have carved the knife to remind him of their time together. It was a gift better than anything Edmund could have imagined.

Smiling, he turned again towards home. The smith had been wrong. You could always trust a Roman who shared some of his apple.

PRAYER: ══

It is easy to be persuaded that strangers are our enemies, so help me not to accept other people's opinions before I have had time to find out that they might be wrong.

Just Like Me

"I wish you were just like me," Samuel said. He was a long and beautiful snake but he didn't have any friends.

"I'm sorry," said William, who was a long and beautiful worm with lots of friends. "I suppose I could change if I really tried."

"I wish you would," Samuel sighed. "And then we could become real friends. We could race over the big meadow and twist ourselves around all the best branches. It would be great if you could change yourself. After all, we're both the same shape, which is a good start."

William liked Samuel a lot, and he thought it would be rather exciting to be able to twist himself around a branch and to swallow eggs as Samuel often did.

"But what do I have to do?" William said. "I'll have to make myself ten times as big if I want to become a snake."

"How should I know?" said Samuel, who had quite a short temper when it came to answering important questions. "Exercises, I suppose, or press-ups."

"What are press-ups?" said William.

Samuel lifted his head and waved the front part of his long body into the air.

"Well, I'll try," said William, doubtfully.

"Six times a day," said Samuel, "and I'll see you next Wednesday."

All that week, William resisted going down through the deep brown layers of soil that he loved so much, and he made himself do press-ups on the garden path in front of the water-butt. So he was quite tired when he met Samuel the following Wednesday as they had arranged.

"Can't see much difference," Samuel said. "You're not even a centimetre bigger or rounder. Try some ordinary stretching exercises and I'll see you next Wednesday."

So all the following week, William lay in the sun and tried to make himself longer, and again he was quite tired when he met Samuel as arranged on the following Wednesday.

"Not a scrap of difference," said Samuel. "Perhaps you should try some creative visualisation."

"Try some - WHAT?" said William, who wasn't very good on long words.

"Try and believe that you're a snake. The mind has great power over the body. You might be very surprised at the results. And make it Thursday next week. It will give you an extra day."

For the whole of the following week, William sat around in the sun telling himself that he was a snake. Some of his friends were quite worried because they hadn't seen him for so long, and several came up out of the soil to check that he was all right.

"Do I look any different?" he asked them.

"A bit tired," said one.

"A bit thinner," said another.

"I've always thought you were a much better brown than the rest of us," said his best friend. "And you still are."

Then they tried to persuade him to go underground again. "We're having a party next Thursday," they said. "The gardener's just made a new compost heap."

"I'm sorry," said William. "I have to meet a friend on Thursday."

So he went on thinking and stretching and doing press-ups until once again, he went to meet Samuel.

"I'm afraid I'm still a worm," he said, "but couldn't we still be friends?"

However, before the snake could reply, the ground was shaken by human footsteps and a voice said, "Got you, my beauty! You're just what I want for my zoo."

Suddenly, William saw his friend lifted by a stick and thrown into a large box. Poor, poor Samuel, he thought, but perhaps he'll make lots of new friends in the zoo. And he was so pleased and happy that he was still a worm that with a quick wriggle, he started to burrow his way back into the golden leaves of the new compost heap just in time for the party.

PRAYER:

Help me not to try to change people into how we would like them to be but to accept them as they are.

Where Did I Put It?

Jane was in a really bad mood. Mum was always asking her to take things around to Mrs Saunders, and every time it took ages because the old lady used to ask her to look for things that she'd lost. She seemed to lose everything - glasses, cardigan, scissors, shopping list - and she would keep losing them over and over again.

"Do I have to take her this?" Jane said, looking at the plate of steak and kidney pudding. "Won't she have cooked her own dinner?"

"I doubt it," said mum. "These days she even forgets to eat. Don't worry, you'll be back before I've finished making the fruit salad."

Jane went around to the back door of the next house, thinking about her friend Bethany who that afternoon was going to show her how to pin up her hair to make her look exactly like their favourite pop star. So it was important that Mrs Saunders didn't delay her by asking her to search for something she'd lost.

She was surprised to find the old lady sitting at the kitchen table which had been neatly laid with a knife and fork and a glass of water.

"I thought you might be coming," Mrs Saunders said. "Your mother is so kind and that pie looks really delicious. You run off now and enjoy your own dinner, and do thank your mother, won't you?"

Jane was delighted to be freed so quickly, and as soon as she and mum had finished their own meal, she was able to go around to Bethany's to get started on the hair straight away.

"We'll shampoo it first," Bethany said. "And then use this conditioner. I sent for it on a special offer, and they've given me this leaflet to show you how to pin it up. I have to check it every time because I keep forgetting which section you start on first."

Very carefully she followed the instructions on the leaflet, and the final result was better than Jane had even hoped for.

"You'll be able to do it yourself next time," Bethany said.

Jane looked doubtful. "Can I borrow the leaflet? Then I can make a copy and give you this one back."

Bethany agreed reluctantly, but she said it would be all right if Jane brought it back to school the next day as she wanted to have another go on her own hair.

When Jane arrived home, however, she found the house full of visitors and her mother in a panic.

"Trust your father to invite his pals around without telling me!" she said. "Can you give me a hand, love? We'll need some more cups and saucers, and you could butter a few scones for me while I make the sandwiches. Your dad said he did tell me, but I think he just forgot," and she bustled away without even looking at Jane's new hair style.

Later when all the excitement was over, Jane remembered Bethany's leaflet. It would be a good chance to copy it now before she did anything else . . . but where had she put it? She could remember putting it in her pocket but it certainly wasn't there now. Nor was it in the hall, or in her bedroom. There wasn't a sign of it in the kitchen or anywhere else.

Perhaps she had dropped it on her way home? However would she be able to tell Bethany that she had lost it?

She slept badly that night, then at breakfast, mum found a letter addressed to Mrs Saunders which had been delivered to them by mistake.

"Slip it around to her now, would you?" said mum. "It won't take you a minute."

It took at least ten, because Mrs Saunders said she had lost her glasses and that the letter might be important and needed to be read right away, so Jane had to help her search all through the house. At last, they found the glasses behind a curtain in the sitting room. It was then that Jane remembered! Dashing home, she went to the sitting room, and there behind a curtain was Bethany's leaflet! She must have popped it there when she went to meet all dad's visitors. Finding it felt as good as being given a Christmas present.

As she was leaving for school, her mum stopped her at the door. "Have you done something to your hair?" she said. "It looks rather nice."

Jane grinned. It was definitely going to be a good day, or as Bethany would say, a good hair day!

PRAYER:

Help me to be patient with old people when they forget where they put things and always to remember how I feel when I lose something.

Holiday Hiccoughs

It was a holiday Maggie won't ever forget. Afterwards she said it could all have gone wrong because of Oliver and his timetables, but he said it was because she was so hopeless at being punctual. Anyway, there they were again, in the same caravan, in the same cliff-top park with mum and dad. Just like they were every August, having the same kind of arguments that they always had whenever Oliver wrote out his timetable for the week.

Maggie had always believed that things were best when you just let them happen, but it was very hard to convince her big brother that they didn't need a timetable to make sure they had a good time. After all, there was her friend, Janet, in the next caravan.

Janet wasn't just there for one week, because she lived there the whole time and her dad actually owned the caravan park. She and Maggie became friends from the first day they met, so both of them were pleased to see each other again.

"Tomorrow we'll go along to Sandy Cove," Janet said. "I want to show you a new path and a cave I found after you'd left last year."

Maggie sighed. "Sorry . . . Oliver's booked tickets for the theme park tomorrow. He did it on the Internet just to show off to mum and dad."

"What about Tuesday?"

"We're going on a coach trip. Oliver's fixed it."

In the end, the only free day Maggie could suggest seemed to be Friday. "We can spend all day together," she said. "But I'll have to be back by five because we're all going to see the show on the pier, and guess who booked that!"

Anyway, although Maggie would never have admitted it, she enjoyed doing all the things Oliver had organised, and the days flew by until at last it was Friday and she was around at Janet's caravan as soon as she'd finished breakfast. Janet's mother had packed them a picnic, and they had a wonderful day of exploring and paddling, and looking for fossils in Sandy Cove.

"Do you realise it's nearly half past four?" Janet said suddenly.

"Oh, we've got ages yet!" said Maggie. "Come on, let's go on a bit further."

She felt she could have walked on forever along the water's edge, searching the glistening sand for the best shells or the most interesting pebbles, and she didn't even want to think about the dreaded thought of packing up and going home the next morning.

When at last, Janet said they ought to go because the tide was coming in, she realised just how tired she was, and what a long climb it was going to be before they reached the cliff tops. It seemed to take hours before they got back to the caravan park.

Maggie's perfect day ended when she saw her mother standing by the door of the caravan. "Where on earth have you been? Do you realise it's half past seven? We've been worried sick!" she said.

Maggie waited for Oliver to come bursting out of the caravan to start complaining about how she had spoilt his timetable, but when she asked where he was, mum said, "He's gone to look for you. He's a bit upset about not seeing the show, but none of us wanted to go until we knew you were safe. He said he couldn't stand around doing nothing."

"It took us ages to get back," Maggie said. She felt awful, knowing how she'd spoilt the end of the holiday for them all. "I'm so sorry, mum," she said. She was about to say it again when she saw Oliver walking back to the caravan. He was with Janet, but instead of looking angry, he was grinning.

"Well, I suppose for once you've just about managed to be on time," he said.

Maggie was puzzled. "I'm sorry. I know it's my fault that we missed the show," she said.

Janet laughed. "Oliver booked for the first performance," she said. "But there's an eight o'clock one as well. My uncle is the stage manager for the pier theatre and I've just telephoned him. They've plenty of seats for eight o'clock. We'll just about make it if we hurry."

And they did. Maggie and Janet sat together in the theatre on the pier, and mum and dad told Oliver that his timetable had been the best one he'd ever done, and no one ever blamed Maggie for being late.

They didn't really need to because she realised how lucky she was to have a friend like Janet who was able to sort everything out.

Maybe in future she would try to be a bit more like Oliver and learn to stick to a timetable. But it wouldn't be easy!

PRAYER:

Help me to try to keep promises and to remember that when I break them, I could affect other people.

Strangers

Mel was the first to notice that the 'For Sale' board on the next door fence had been replaced by a 'Sold' one.

"That's nice," said mum, when Mel ran into the house to tell her. "We shall have new neighbours at last."

Each day during the summer, Mel had crept through the fence between the houses and pretended that the lawn next door was a real jungle. Now strangers were going to live there, and nothing would be the same any more, but it wasn't until August that a big removal van pulled up at the gate.

"They've had a long journey," said mum. "I'm sure they'd like some tea."

Mel often felt embarrassed with mum who was always offering to do things for people, and she often talked to people she met in shops and to people she didn't even know. But there was nothing that Mel could do about it, so she kept out of sight as mum carried a tray with tea and biscuits into the empty house next door. Mum was gone for ages. Then she came back looking very pleased and said, "You'll have some new friends. There's a girl called Clare, and two boys, Jack and William."

"I don't like strangers," said Mel. "Besides, I don't need any new friends. I've got enough already."

All through that weekend she could hear the new neighbours laughing and talking in the garden, but by Monday she forgot all about them because Prinny had gone missing again. Mel had chosen her from all the others at the Cats' Home and had called her Princess because she was so beautiful. But Prinny was a wanderer and was always going missing. This time there was no sign of her for more than a week even though Mel pinned up notices in all the shops.

"Don't worry," said mum. "She'll come back when she's ready."

Then, when they were having breakfast one morning, there was a ring at the door and when Mel opened it, three children were standing there, one of them holding a purring Prinny in his arms.

"We read your notice in the Post Office," said one of the boys. "We had a white cat once so we know how special they are."

His sister pushed him aside. "We've only just found her. She was in our tent in the garden. We left a pile of dressing up clothes out there and she must have slept there last night. She looks a bit thin but I think she's all right."

Mum had come to the door now and was as excited as Mel. "Prinny! Where on earth have you been all this time? Sorry, William, do come in. Mel, find some chairs for everybody and I'll make some more toast."

So the children from next door joined Mel at the breakfast table and later some of her other friends came round too. Soon everybody knew everybody else. Clare told Mel about her rabbits and asked her if she'd like to go round to see them, and the boys invited her to look at the tent that Prinny had liked so much. In fact, Mel spent the whole day at their house and told mum afterwards that it was one of the best days she'd ever had.

"I thought you didn't like strangers," said mum.

"They're not strangers," said Mel. "They're called Clare, Jack and William and they're my friends."

Sometimes, she thought, mums can say some really stupid things.

PRAYER:

Help me to remember that making new friends is never as difficult as we think it's going to be.

Summer with Gran

Lottie had often stayed with Gran before. It was always in the summer when you could hardly see Gran's cottage for all the long grass and the honeysuckle climbing around its front door. Going on her own without Andrew and the twins was what made the holiday so special. Her little brother Andrew was a nuisance. He was always banging into things or falling over and hurting himself, and if the twins had gone, it would have meant that mum would have had to go too, because they were only twelve months old. Anyway, Gran had only one tiny spare bedroom and this was why Lottie always went on her own.

Lottie loved everything about Gran's cottage except for the moths. She didn't mind them in the garden in daylight, but when it was dusk they would come through the tiny window in the thatched roof and flutter towards Lottie and the little bedside lamp. Lottie would quickly switch off the light and dive under the sheets until the moths had flown out into the darkness again.

She had never told anyone about this, but even just thinking about them fluttering close to her face, made her feel shivery and strange.

This year, when mum read out Gran's invitation to come and stay, Lottie was horrified to hear that Andrew would be coming with her for the week's holiday.

"He might not have another chance," mum explained. "Gran doesn't think she'll be able to cope with the cottage on her own for much longer. So she's going to put up a little camp bed in the spare room so that you and Andrew can enjoy going there together."

However, once the holiday had begun, Lottie found that she enjoyed showing her brother all the secret places of Gran's garden, and taking him down to the stream to see if they could find any of the frogs she'd found there before.

It was at bedtime on the first night, that Andrew began to be a nuisance. He started crying just as he did at home, and he made Gran go up and down the stairs with drinks of water. Gran told Lottie that it was only because he was missing his own bed, and she went downstairs again and found the special little car that he liked to sleep with.

When they were on their own again, Andrew went on sobbing, and Lottie wished that she was still on her own as she always had been before. Then suddenly, before she had time to switch off the light, she saw two large moths fluttering and banging themselves against the lampshade. Andrew began to scream.

"Get Gran!" he shouted. "Go and get Gran. I don't like the big ones."

Lottie thought of Gran's slow climb up the stairs and of how tired she had looked when they came in from their evening walk down the lane.

"It's all right," Lottie said. "They're only moths. They won't hurt you."

Jumping out of bed, she took her towel from the back of the chair, and gently guiding the moths out of the window, she said, "If you stop crying, I'll tell you a story about that frog I showed you this afternoon."

Andrew looked happy again, and he listened to her quietly until, by the time she had finished the story, she saw that he had fallen asleep.

Suddenly she began to feel happy too, and thought of how she would tell Gran about what she had done to help the moths find their way out into the garden again.

Nothing now was going to spoil this special holiday, even if it meant that she had to share it with Andrew. After all, you can hardly expect a three year old to understand about moths and things like that, can you?

PRAYER:

Help me to be brave enough to face the things that make me afraid.

Tolly the Tortoise

Even now Shelley isn't quite sure if it was all a dream.

She can clearly remember the clock chiming, so what happened afterwards must have been real, because the clock is a real one. It sits on the small table in the hall, and she can hear it very clearly when she's upstairs and tucked up in bed.

It had been a very ordinary school day, except for Lisa, who seemed to be getting worse. It was all right when Lisa was the new girl. After all, you don't expect someone new to go around chatting to everybody, but it was now six months since Shelley first sat next to Lisa in Class 2, and still she hardly said a word.

Shelley knew you had to be friendly when someone was new, but it was hopeless trying to be friends with Lisa. After today, Shelley had decided that in future she wouldn't even bother to speak to her again. She was still thinking about this as she got into bed.

Then the clock chimed and she heard a noise. It was an odd, scuffling, scurrying sort of noise, and then there was a puffing noise as if someone was trying to struggle out of a tight jumper. Then the puffing stopped and she heard a scuttle of tiny feet across the floor. Shelley sat up quickly, and there, sitting at the foot of the bed, was a tiny wrinkled creature. It was covered with dark, leathery skin, which hung from its shoulders in hundreds of folds and creases.

"Why don't you say something?" it said. "Surely you can recognise your own tortoise when it's in front of you?"

Shelley gasped. "Are you Tolly?" she said. "But where's your shell? Won't you catch a cold like that?"

Tolly frowned, making two more wrinkles across his tiny forehead. "Never mind all that. Are you ready?"

Shelley put out her hand and found herself gliding through the door into a long, watery corridor full of tall swaying weeds. As they hurried along, two goldfish glided by them, each opening its mouth silently as it passed.

"How unfriendly of them not to speak," said Shelley, producing seven large bubbles that floated gracefully out of her mouth.

"Didn't you recognise them?" said Tolly. "They're the ones you keep in that round bowl on the sideboard."

Not wanting to make any more bubbles, Shelley didn't reply.

"Did you say something?" said Tolly.

"Er no . . . I was thinking." She spoke softly, and five smaller bubbles floated away in front of her. "Perhaps they ought to be in a large tank," she said, which produced another nine rather larger bubbles.

"Good, I'm glad you're learning," said Tolly. "We don't always have to use words to make ourselves understood. In fact words often make things more difficult. Thinking is much more important. Now then, here we are. I hope you like circuses."

All Shelley could see was a big round empty space. "It doesn't look much like a circus," she said.

"If you will allow it to be a circus," Tolly said, "you will find it will become a circus. The trouble with you is that you never let things be themselves. Ah, now it's beginning. Tiger-fish. Very well trained, and all done by kindness."

Shelley watched in amazement. The six fierce Tiger-fish were followed by two fat old goldfish wearing funny hats, and then a trapeze act where four Chinese fish, which balanced on the end of their tails, swayed their way between the tall reeds. Then followed a finale of minnows riding sea-horses, until at last Tolly said, "Time to go. That's if I can remember where I put my shell . . . ah, yes, I think I remember.'"

His voice seemed to fade as Shelley heard the clock chiming downstairs in the hall.

"Tolly?" she said. But she saw that it was daylight, and the room was empty.

Dressing quickly, she hurried to the kitchen and then out into the garden to Tolly's favourite spot under the hollyhocks. With relief she saw the patterned mound of his shell, and when she lifted him, he stretched out his head as he always did.

"It was a lovely circus," she said, "but you look much better in your shell."

Tolly said nothing, and she remembered what he had said about thinking being better than talking. Even if it had been a dream, she knew one thing. She certainly had a very wise and unusual tortoise!

PRAYER:

Help me to understand that some people find it difficult to use words easily and might need our help to bring them "out of their shell."